FONDUE MAGIC:

Fun, Flame and Saucery
Around the World

FONDUE MAGIC:

Fun, Flame and Saucery
Around the World

BY ANITA PRICHARD

Illustrated by Zue Martin

HEARTHSIDE PRESS INCORPORATED
Publishers • New York

Contents

I dedicate this book to my sister Jean, whose professional advice started and encouraged me in a new and exciting secondary career of writing, and also to my editor, Nedda Casson Anders, whose close and patient collaboration with me in all aspects of this book made its completion possible.

Let me also express my gratitude to Libby Hillman, knowledgable cuisinière and author of two of my favorite cookbooks, for her many kindnesses and unflaggingly cheerful support. I want to acknowledge the help of my stewardess friends, Sharlotte Jones and Shirley Groshardt, who have long made fondue cooking an integral part of their at-home entertaining, and the assistance, as well, of Nancy, Book, and Rosemary Heslin and of Jean O'Rourke, all of whom contributed party recipes to this book. Especially warm thanks go to Dennis Durian and his roommates at the University of Dayton, who helped bridge the generation gap by acting as my official tasters.

I'm indebted to gourmets Captain J. J. Smith (retired), Frank Tillman, R. J. Sparks, Leslie Renfield and Fred Waller for the masculine point of view, as well as for their special recipes, contributed to the cause of international cuisine. My appreciation, in abundance, goes to two great cooks from Tennessee, Mrs. Leslie Oakley and the late Mrs. Harry Martin, Sr., authorities on early American cookery. And, for her sympathetic and deft assistance with the manuscript, I add my thanks to Janet Lauren of Hearthside Press.

Publishers' Note: When Is a Fondue?

Let us define our terms, as the scholars say. What is a fondue, and who is doing the defining? In view of the contemporary wave of interest in, and excitement over, fondue cookery and entertaining, we feel fully justified in re-evaluating and extending the classic concepts.

As by now practically everybody knows, "fondue" is the past participle of the French verb *fondre*, meaning to melt. The old-fashioned American baked cheese fondue had its counterpart in Brillat-Savarin's recipe for *fondue au fromage*, a dish made of melted cheese and scrambled eggs. But the Swiss classic that started the current vogue is *fondue* de *fromage*, in which melted Swiss cheese (Gruyère, Emmentaler, or both) is combined with a whisper of garlic, pepper, dry wine, and kirsch. We bow low to the classic Swiss fondue, and you'll find it given the full treatment here.

But by extension, witness the beef fondue known as Fondue Bourguignonne, whose pedigree (even if fabled) and many variations will also be explored in this book. The fact is that a fondue has come to mean any bubbling melted or liquid substance, sometimes prepared but *always* kept heated at the table, in which one dips or cooks other foods. In short, the cooking-by-dunking technique. In a charming German treatise on this whole subject, an entire chapter is devoted to "Schwindlerei" or Little Swindles— i.e., fake fondues. Well, if to the purist any fondue that is not cheese is a fake, *Fondue Magic* abounds in swindles. But our position is clear. We are all for including the chocolate fondue and the many variations of Mexican, Italian, Hawaiian, Japanese, American *et al* dishes that meet with the above-stated primary requirement: you prepare a simmering something to be kept hot atop a fondue burner, and into it you dip or spear a host of dunkables, to sop up, or be cooked in, the molten whatever. This, in essence, is our free interpretation of fondue. The store windows are full of fondue pots—every type and size. We strongly suspect you've got one or will have one shortly, and if this book inveigles you into using it in every possible delightful and life-lightening way, we'll have achieved our purpose.

Introduction

Once upon a time, a lonely Swiss shepherd, tending his flocks on a precipitous and isolated Alpine slope, sat down to eat his customary meal of bread, cheese and wine.

"My God!" (or perhaps "Mein Gott!" if he was in a German-speaking canton, which is more than likely), he exclaimed. "I simply cannot *face* this stuff AGAIN. There *must* be ein anderer Weg!" And so, in sheer desperation, he lit a fire under his iron pot (standard item of shepherd equipment) and did something that was to shake the food world to its foundations: he melted the cheese and wine together in the heated pot, and then dunked his sturdy peasant bread in the mixture.

This, so legend has it, was the first fondue. I'm not of a mind to dispute it. The Swiss, after all, in addition to making first-class cuckoo-clocks, growing edelweiss and yodeling are ardent dunkers, starting in the morning with hot chocolate, and dipping away steadily through after-dinner coffee.

How did any of this come to involve or interest *me*, the product of the sturdy southern-tinged American cuisine of my rural Indiana forebears? Par avion, as they say. I had become an airline stewardess, moved to New York—and you know what *that* means. Alien influences. Growth and liberation. Well-met chance acquaintances. One of whom was a bachelor friend who, at a given moment in both of our lives, found himself driving through a treacherous Swiss mountain pass (they are *always* treacherous, hence the St. Bernard) on a foggy night in the 1950's. Suddenly a rustic inn emerged, as is its quaint custom, out of the blurred landscape, and the weary traveler soon found himself sitting before a cozy fire tasting one of the established delights of Alpine cuisine, cheese fondue. The shepherd had gotten the word around, you see.

When my far-flung acquaintance returned to our home hamlet, New York, he asked me to roust up a recipe that would duplicate this tasty dish. I found nothing remotely comparable, and decided to research Swiss fondue head-on.

Remember, I'm in the air business. I planned a European grand tour, to include Switzerland, with a few extra-curricular projects in mind. I found the natives amazingly friendly. I was given a warm welcome, a Swiss watch, and lots of fondues, of which the Alpine dwellers are understandably proud. And we must remember that before sports-minded Europeans turned the lofty snow-covered peaks into tourist sporting terrain, these isolated mountain-and-valley people were accustomed to make do, during the long winters, with a diet of bread, potatoes, and a big wheel of cheese.

The European ski buffs were joined, after the War, by like-minded Americans, and Switzerland became the playground of well-heeled folk in avid search of pleasure and good food. And in the elaborate ski lodges that sprang up all over the snow-capped land, the poverty diet of the mountain dweller became the party fare of the international traveler.

Which, of course, is what I myself was, in the 1950's— and from my subsequent international recipe sleuthing expeditions emerged the fact that most national cuisines have evolved at least *one* dish similar and/or adaptable to the fondue formula.

Whence these recipes and menus, suitable for a rich variety of Fun Fondue parties planned for a group of six unless otherwise noted. Why is six the magic number? It's simply that most fondue pots are appropriately sized to accommodate six at the festive board; the number approximates that of the average family, or grouping of three couples. More than six—a baker's dozen? No problem: *two* fondue pots, one at each end of the table.

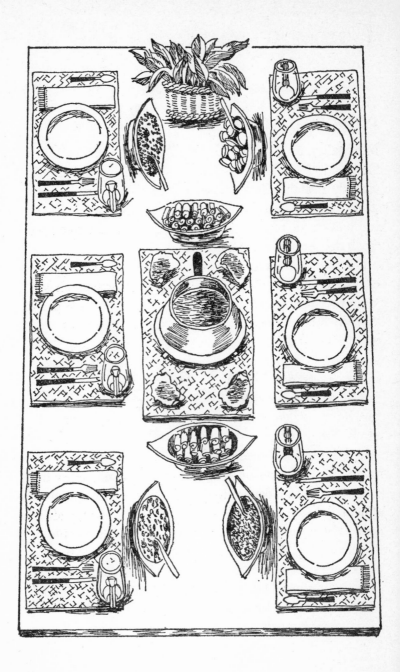

I HOW TO GO ABOUT IT

INFORMALITY UBER ALLES

Informality, *au fond* as well as *au fondue,* is really all in the mind. I say this because of the widespread notion (grossly mistaken in my opinion) that "informal" means slacks for the girls, no ties for the gents, paper plates, and feet up all 'round. The informality of the fondue goes much deeper and is far more genuine.

Whether you number six or twelve (i.e., one pot or two), there's more to the fondue than its gustatory charm. A hot dish to start with, it invariably proves to be a party ice-breaker, capable of thawing the glacial surface of even the Person Nobody Knows. You simply can't stay aloof from people who are dunking and dipping alongside of you. Conversations are kindled, and spread like the proverbial wildfire, sparked with quick wit and gay repartee (provided, of course, that your guests are potentially quick-witted and reparteeing types).

In addition to being a conversational catalyst, the fondue is also marvelously versatile, adaptable across the menu from hors d'oeuvre to dessert; an appetite-stimulant at noon (cheese, perhaps), it's wickedly good in the afternoon (chocolate fondue, for example)—and delectable in the wee hours. It makes for a heaven-sent after-theatre supper—despite white tie and tails—because it can be prepared in jig-time. And, granted that a cheese fondue served with cocktails is a bit much, it lends itself wonderfully to late Sunday brunch, preceded by a bullshot or a Bloody

Mary. And for the ritual American "informal supper," especially one prepared by the careerist just home from a nine-hour office stint complete with commute, the fondue is literally nonpareil.

No matter what the guests may be wearing (clothing suggestions appear elsewhere in this volume), forget your fancy table appointments when you plan a fondue party. Your tablecloth had best be washable, or else cook on a table surface (equally suitable setting) that wipes clean without giving you an argument: although most fondue pots should be set on trays, there is no way of avoiding a certain amount of splatter and drip.

Cardinal Rule, repeated like an incantation in the pages that follow: place the fondue pot in the center of the table, within easy reach of each guest. Save your tasteful floral arrangements for Another Time. Put a dinner plate in front of each person. And if you're serving a meat fondue, and happen to be blessed with a supply of plates having separate compartments, now's the time to haul them down and use them.

A non-rule for table arrangers: there's no one correct placement for flatware. Peripatetic dunkers are just as likely to find skewers, and fondue and dinner forks, on the right of, or right-angled above, the dinner plate, as on the left of it.

Again, for meat fondues, you can arrange a batch of sauce bowls artistically around the fondue burner. My own special pets are the 5½-inch mother-of-pearl shell boats from the Philippines. But any small bowl or shell set will do nicely.

As to the sauces themselves, to be dipped into in a subsequent chapter—the field is yours! A variety of sauces as well as relishes, mustard and tartar are all suitable embellishments. I personally make my own sauces, and am including a number of my own recipes, but specialty food departments offer an enticing assortment, and they'll do nicely if they must.

To go with the next course, assuming you're being ambitious, serve a simple salad and a good crusty bread, homemade if you have the time (see the special supplement on sourdough and quick batter breads). If you haven't ,and many don't, pick up a loaf, Italian or French style, on your way home. Just make sure you serve it hot. For dessert, I recommend a simple fruit compote, or a fruit flambé, which will utilize the fondue burner and any attractive flameproof skillet that fits over it. Just as appropriate, however, and unbeatably good, is a bowl of fresh fruit in season.

So, to complete the table setting, you'll want rustic table accessories—earthenware, copper, wooden or pewter bowls and platters, a straw basket for bread and a crock for butter, and informal flatware. Suggested color: bright, gay. Added provocative note: napkins folded in the European manner (ideas for napkin-folding may be found in many sections of this book) and tucked into wine goblets. (Caution: remove before pouring.) So much for the setting; now to the nitty-gritty.

FONDUE EQUIPMENT: WHAT DO YOU NEED?

One crucial preliminary word of caution on the subject of acquiring fondue equipment: don't dash out and buy. Proceed slowly and with care. Unless somebody's presented you with a top-quality kit, it's a steep investment and you will not want to go wrong. And you *can.* Many fondue fans subscribe to the naïve notion that the choice of utensils is a matter of taste and budget.

Not so. The U. S. market is presently glutted with inexpensive imports of poorly tempered metal that lacks the hardness and resiliency to withstand intense heat. One fondue pot actually burst into a spectacular blaze at the table, because the heated cooking oil (this was a meat fondue) so increased the temperature of the metal that a grease fire broke out. Beware.

In the interest of safety as well as of cuisine, buy your fondue equipment from a reputable manufacturer, one who'll stand behind his guarantee. If he's worth his melted cheese, he'll include, as well, explicit instructions as to the cleaning and care of his product.

SELECTING A FONDUE POT

Earthenware, metal, and enamel-covered cast-iron pots all are available. In days of yore, the Swiss used the earthenware *caquelon.* To this day, a venerable pottery factory in Switzerland exports earthenware fondue pots and accessories adorned with charming primitive motifs. But today, most of the Swiss have converted to metal (our metallic age!) because it can accommodate both beef and cheese fondues. Earthenware pottery, which is splendid for cheese and chocolate, may crack at the high temperature required for proper preparation of a beef fondue; the metal, by contrast, *can* be used for cheese and chocolate provided the temperature is controlled and kept low —and is ideal for the hot oil cookery required for the meat fondues. Highly decorative and durable cast-iron pots covered with enamel, imported chiefly from Belgium, France, Switzerland and Holland, handle cheese, meat and chocolate fondues with equal aplomb.

Recently introduced by Oster is an electric fondue set consisting of a Teflon-lined metal fondue pot and electric heating unit. Because of the controlled heat of the electric fondue, all three kinds of fondue can be prepared and served in the same pot.

FONDUE BURNERS

No burner on the table, no fondue. You can select from a variety of burners and burner fuels. These latter include denatured alcohol, found in hardware stores; you'll pour it into your burner prior to lighting. Or you can use sterno, small cans of which are available at most grocery and hardware stores. Another variety of burner uses propane gas for fuel. The electric fondue units are equipped with dials for thermostatic control of heat, from very low to very high.

In this book all temperature settings are given as low, medium and high. If your electric fondue control has numbers, low setting includes numbers 1-4, medium 5-7, high 8-9. It may be necessary to adjust control within a temperate range to keep fondues at the right consistency.

Have you heard terrifying tales of sudden fire at the table? Be reassured: most burners on today's market have a flameproof insert. But don't become *over*-reassured; *no* burner can be rendered automatically non-inflammable. You must exert real care in the filling and refilling; remember always to wipe off all traces of fluid from the burner before you light it. Even the electric burners must be handled carefully, as the oil used for beef cooking can heat up to 400°F.

FONDUE ACCESSORIES

A fondue pot is necessarily rather deep; for some types of cooking—flambées, for example—shallow flameproof skillets can replace them. Use one that's decorative, with a handle that won't be a heat conductor. For an outsized party, with too many guests to be accommodated by even the contents of two regular fondue pots, cheese fondue can be made in the kitchen in a simple double boiler, and then transferred to the table pot or pots. Most of the time, of course, you'll want to fondue in the fondue pot, and not mess with other cookware. If you really take fondues to your heart and make them an integral part of home entertaining, you can go hogwild on accessories. For a cheese fondue, you can stock up on service plates, with schnapps cups for kirsch or other brandies. Meat fondues, as will be discussed in due course, are usually accompanied by a veritable galaxy of sauces, egging (watch that metaphor!) you on to the purchase of small bowls, condiment dishes, or even a lazy susan.

FONDUE FORKS AND SKEWERS

A cheese fondue fork, which serves the relatively simple function of dipping chunks of bread into the frothing cheese, is two-pronged, and has grooved handles. With meat fondues, skewers rather than forks are the traditional utensil, the theory being that skewered meat will adhere more tenaciously while cooking in the fat, a somewhat longer process. Fondue metal meat skewers are available in sets of six. The skewered, cooked meat is transferred to one's dinner plate, and then eaten with a regular fork.

For large buffet parties, wooden forks and "barbecue sticks" are indispensables, especially if it's cheese and chocolate that's being dipped into.

The final word on this entire subject simply reiterates my opening remarks: discretion is the better part of value as you start your new life and times with fondue. Buy equipment cautiously, then buy the best the market affords. And with fondue equipment, alas, as with so many other material things, the best is, usually, if not invariably, the most expensive.

FONDUE COOKERY CLUES: CHEESE, BEEF, CHOCOLATE ET AL

CHEESE FONDUES

1. Don't proceed piecemeal. Read the recipe thoroughly, and assemble all ingredients in advance. Once you start, you won't want to stop and ponder. Fondues are fast.

2. Don't rely upon an alcohol flame to preheat the pot for you; this must be accomplished in the kitchen on the stove, and the preheated pot then brought to the table. Follow instructions of manufacturer for use of electric burners and butane gas.

3. Warm the wine in the cooking pot over low heat; then put in the first one-third of your cheese. Start stirring in a figure-8 motion, adding the remaining cheese gradually.

4. Keep the cheese mixture at a uniformly hot temperature, so that it cooks at a slow bubble or simmer. If you do this, the fondue won't become tough, but will achieve the desirable molten, sauce-like consistency.

5. (Repetitious but added for emphasis, as this can make or break your fondue): A cheese fondue *must* cook over a very low heat, or it'll become stringy. Disastrous.

6. If the cheese/wine mixture doesn't thicken, or if the mixture starts to separate, take the following emergency measure: put it back on the stove, whip briskly with a wire whisk, and add ½ teaspoon cornstarch.

7. If you've done this faithfully, and the fondue remains lumpy, don't conclude that it's you who are to blame; it could just be the cheese. Emphasis throughout this book is placed on the importance of mature, naturally aged cheese because cheese that hasn't matured properly tends to get stringy or lumpy. The surest way of avoiding this unhappy eventuality is to use a natural aged cheese, and *not* a processed one.

8. If the fondue becomes too thick, back to the stove with it. Thin the mixture by adding some *warmed* wine—just enough to enable you to maintain what should now be a creamy consistency.

9. Steps 2 through 8 can be simplified by using the new Oster Electric Fondue and the blender. To make cheese fondues, heat liquid in electric fondue pot over medium heat until bubbles start to rise to the surface. Put all remaining ingredients into the blender container. Cheese does not have to be grated—just cubed. Add heated liquid, cover and process at highest speed until smooth. If recipe calls for eggs, add them last while blending to prevent curdling. Pour into electric fondue pot and cook over medium heat until mixture is heated and bubbly. Reduce heat to keep cheese at a slow bubble or simmer. If fondue becomes too thick while serving, gradually add heated liquid while stirring briskly.

BEEF FONDUES

1. As to the matter of oil: Use peanut oil (French if available) or a quality corn oil. *Don't* use olive oil or butter: the former tends to impose its own flavor on the food you're cooking—beef in particular—and butter will burn, sure's fire. A teaspoon of salt in the fondue pot will help reduce splatters.

2. Fill your fondue pot about halfway: 3 cups or so in the average pan. Preheat oil to 375°F., or until a 1½-inch cube of bread browns in 30-40 seconds. Follow manufacturer's directions for heating oil. In an electric fondue pot, the oil can be heated right at the table over the electric unit and maintained at a proper temperature during the fondue feast.

3. Handle hot oil with utmost caution!

4. If the oil starts to cool at the table, bring it to the boiling point once more. You can do this right at the table in an electric pot; follow manufacturer's directions for other kinds.

5. The oil can be used again. After the fondue, let the fat cool, then strain it through cheesecloth, paper towels or a fine sieve, clarify, and store covered in the refrigerator until needed. (To clarify oil, brown, slowly, several slices of raw potatoes in hot oil.)

6. Unless you are using an electric fondue, no more than 3 guests should dip at one time; if too many dip, the temperature of the oil is lowered. Bring it to the proper temperature once more on the kitchen range.

7. Have meats at room temperature before frying. To avoid spattering, blot off excess moisture, especially if meat has been frozen.

CHOCOLATE FONDUES

See the detailed instructions given in Chapter VI, Section 14, Chocolate Fondues (Sweet and Bitter).

These extremely general and basic instructions cover most of the fondues discussed in our book. Special fondues such as bagna cauda and variations of meat fondues will be clarified, when there's any significant deviation from these hints, as we go along.

II SWITZERLAND, Fondue Homeland: Cantons and Concoctions

There are two essentials to bear in mind—perhaps three—as we approach Switzerland in her role as the motherland of the fondue (cheese in particular). First, Switzerland, together with its Alpine terrain, is full of the richest kind of high pastureland, where contented cows munch succulent grasses, and where people like Heidi's grandfather still coddle their well-foddered cattle with tender loving care, milk by hand with stools and pails—and are past masters in the art of cheese-making. What's internationally marketed as Swiss cheese is the least part of it, as we'll see.

Second, Switzerland (as if you need be reminded) is essentially a three-language, three-culture country, bordered by Germany to the North, France to the West, Austria to the South East, and Italy to the South. In addition to the patois known as Swiss, three languages are spoken in this tiny land, and three distinct cultures are reflected in its inhabitants, architecture, culture and cuisine.

And third, partly because of its internationalism and partly, too, because of Swiss efficiency, Switzerland has become *the* center of the hotel and innkeeping profession, annually exporting thousands of its superbly trained hotel-school graduates to run establishments all over the world. Switzerland knows about food—how to make it and serve it.

What better place to start on a fact-finding fondue safari?

So, as stated earlier, I took myself off to Switzerland in 1956, in the pre-jet age, when you could still travel at a leisurely pace and set your own itinerary without making reservations through travel agents eighteen months in advance. Switzerland is, of course, a wonderful wanderer's paradise, ideal for day-long sightseeing tours through breathtakingly beautiful countryside. Distances are relatively small; the pace changes from canton to canton. Swiss travel is an excursion into varied wonderlands of weather, scenic delights, people, dialects—and fondues. From crystal-clear lakes bounded by snow-capped mountains of glacial grandeur, with valleys and village inns tucked amongst them, to the elegance of cosmopolitan Zurich, one can eat one's way through a gourmet assortment of fondues. In this chapter I'll deal with seven classics, together with the circumstances under which I encountered them, and the meals (menus and recipes included) of which they were the stellar attraction.

1. THE BASIC CHEESE FONDUE, A ZURICH SPECIALTY

The basic cheese fondue, as we think of it here in the United States, is actually a specialty of Zurich and its surrounding districts. Particularly characteristic of the region is the distinctive habit of twirling the cubed bread in the kirsch before dunking it in the fondue. This charming custom, now eagerly accepted everywhere, carries with it its own special consequences: if a lady, in the course of dunking, loses her bread in the fondue, she pays the kind of forfeit that's bound to catch on internationally: a kiss to the nearest man. If it's a man whose bread-cube gets away, he provides the next bottle of wine. (Men seem universally agreeable to both aspects of this arrangement.) For obvious reasons, it's not considered good form to cheat, i.e., to deliberately unprong anybody else's bread.

This first basic cheese fondue is listed as the nucleus of an After-Theatre Fondue Supper because a Zurich waiter, wise in the ways of Americans and their endless cocktail parties, suggested that I forego scheduling the fondue as a post-cocktail dinner dish, where its charms would be dissipated by everybody's being a bit looped and much too full of canapés—and that I serve it late, as an after-theatre or sledding-party treat, by which time everyone would be both sober and ravenous. Wine and kirsch are entrenched parts of the fondue ritual, but the Swiss feel strongly that even cold beer, let alone a dry martini, will turn the fondue into a glutinous mass once it reaches the stomach. I report this for precisely what it's worth, but that's how I got it from the Zurich waiter, and there's much to be said for his point of view.

You'll note that we end, not merely with Swiss coffee, but with Swiss Coffee Dunk. "Dunken" is a variant on the German "tunken" which means, literally, to dip, to steep, above all to *sop* (bread, etc.) in a fluid and eat it. The Swiss traditionally end the cheese fondue ritual by soaking sugar cubes in whatever kirsch is left over in the schnapps cups. They then (like the Russians with their tea) place the soaked sugar cubes between their front teeth, and filter their black coffee through the liqueur-drenched sweet. A delectable final note.

MENU

Cheese Fondue, (Zurich-style)—recipe follows
Toasted Cubes of French or Italian Bread
Wine: Neuchâtel—Kirsch
Pineapple Surprise: Cut 2 small pineapples into halves to
   form 4 shells, or quarter 1 large pineapple to form 4
   shells. Using a sharp knife, remove the fruit without
   cutting the rind. Cut the pineapple in bite-size chunks.
   Sweeten if necessary by sprinkling with fine sugar. Pour
   ½ cup kirsch over cubes. Heat thoroughly. Blend in 1
   cup of coarsely chopped butternut or filbert crunch just
   before serving. Place a scoop of ice cream in each pineapple shell. Cover with the heated pineapple mixture
   and serve immediately. Serves 4.
Frosted Grapes: Wash 3 bunches of grapes (assorted
   colors), about 2 pounds. Drain and chill. Beat 1 egg
   white until frothy, but not stiff. Brush grapes with a
   pastry brush dipped in the egg white; sprinkle with the
   granulated sugar. Let stand on a rack until dry. Arrange
   artistically. Serves 4.
Swiss Coffee Dunk

CHEESE FONDUE, Zurich-style

   1 clove fresh garlic
   2 cups dry white wine (Neuchâtel, Moselle or Rhine)
   1 tablespoon lemon juice
   1 pound aged Swiss cheese (Emmentaler), grated or finely minced
   3 tablespoons flour
   3 tablespoons kirsch
   ¼ teaspoon nutmeg
      Dash of paprika

PART I (IN ADVANCE):

Rub fondue pot with garlic. Discard garlic. Pour wine in fondue pot. Set over moderate heat. Heat the wine but do not boil, add lemon juice. Toss cheese with the flour and add by handfuls, ⅓ at a time, stirring constantly with a wooden fork or spoon until cheese is melted. Bring fondue to a bubble briefly (a few seconds), add kirsch, nutmeg and paprika, stirring until blended.

PART II (FONDUE POT OVER TABLE BURNER;
USE MEDIUM SETTING ON ELECTRIC FONDUE):

Adjust the burner so that the fondue will simmer slowly throughout the meal.

PART III (EACH GUEST):

Spears a cube of bread through soft side of crust, twirls it in schnapps cup of kirsch, and then dunks it into the pot, giving a good stir each time. *Note:* Towards the end of the meal, the cheese gets crusty at the bottom of the fondue pot. The crust is considered a delicacy and should be evenly divided among the diners. Serves 4 as main dish or 10-12 as appetizer.

Variations: Add 1 cup puréed cooked spinach or tomato to Part I of the basic recipe.

2. IN GENEVA THE ACCENT IS GALLIC

My Swiss saunterings next took me to Geneva, venerable capital of the French sector. Despite its austere religious historic role as the stamping (and stamping out) ground of fervent Reformist John Calvin and his zealous followers, Geneva is one of the most beguilingly lovely cities in all of Europe. After a day of traipsing about the lake and mountain area, where the cool, crisp, high-altitude air puts an edge on the most jaded appetite, I came back to my hotel, starved, of course, and asked my friendly concierge (the man most likely to be of help on almost any count in any country) where I might find a restaurant that served a first-class cheese fondue.

Accordingly, that evening I dined at Le Palais de Justice (potential voyagers please make note), 8 Place du Bourg-deFour. This informal restaurant, which resembles a barrel-vaulted cave, provided, even in September when the weather was too balmy for skiing, a temperature nippy enough to enhance the tasty delight of the fondue ritual.

I feel free, always and everywhere, to plunge into conversation with concierges and waiters; I questioned my man at Le Palais de Justice, who seemed genuinely pleased by my curiosity, and he divulged the following folklore about the crucial role that wine plays in the fondue ritual, to wit:

In Switzerland, during the long winter evenings, one of the national pastimes is to sit around the earthenware "caquelon," swirling pieces of bread in a cheese fondue. This can scarcely be regarded as light fare. Au contraire. Consequently, the Swiss wisely compensate by drinking nothing with their winter's night meal except a dry white wine, and/or kirsch, or hot tea. I, who had rarely seen Swiss wines on sale in New York stores, was astounded by the variety and excellence of the Swiss vintages. However, as is the case with some of the most delightful local wines in other countries, Swiss wines are at their best when tasted on native soil. They don't export well.

The white Neuchâtel wines are light, sparkling, and a perfect refreshing foil for cheese fondue. (Experts state that the criterion of a superior Neuchâtel is that it form a star in the glass as it's poured from the bottle.) Other suggested wines that serve as fine complements to fondue are the Rhine and Moselle wines from the nearby German vineyards, which date back to the days of the Holy Roman Empire.

The famous kirsch, to which we've already made frequent reference, is distilled from cherry seeds, and it's a very potent spirit indeed. There are those who consider kirsch a basic ingredient in the concocting of an authentic cheese fondue, but even in Switzerland this isn't necessarily true: some cantons don't use kirsch at all; others substitute cognac, light rum, or applejack. Sugar-cubes dunk equally well in all of these. In Geneva, the fondue is likely to be made, as my recipe indicates, with eggs and champagne.

Back to my menu. Bear in mind that despite the reference just above to German vineyards nearby (everything is "nearby" in Switzerland), the 109 square miles occupied by the canton of which Geneva is the capital is almost entirely surrounded by France, and dotted with vineyards and orchards; the people, of course, speak French, follow French customs, and eat French food. Hence the strongly Gallic flavor of the fondue and of the soup which precedes it. It would be unthinkable to write even the smallest dissertation on French cooking in Geneva without mentioning the onion soup!

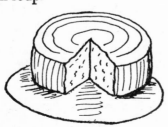

MENU

Soup à l'oignon (onion soup): Melt 1½ teaspoons butter and 1 tablespoon French olive oil in a saucepan. Add 1 pound minced onions and sauté for 15 minutes. Add a pinch of sugar which will give the soup a rich golden color. Sprinkle 1 tablespoon flour over the onions and gradually add 1 quart hot beef bouillon or broth and then stir in 2 tablespoons Armagnac or cognac. Continue to stir until the mixture is well blended. Allow the soup to simmer for 45 minutes. Transfer the soup to individual bowls and serve at once. Serves 4.

Cheese Fondue (Geneva Style)—recipe follows

Cubes of French or Italian Bread

Wine: Mumm's Cordon Rouge or Almaden Brut

French Green Salad with Mustard Dressing: Separate leaves of 3 heads Belgian endive. Chill. Remove dark green outer leaves of 2 heads Boston lettuce and discard. Wash remaining lettuce, drain well, wrap in paper toweling, and crisp in refrigerator. (*Note:* the following may be done by host at table): In a large wooden salad bowl, blend 2 tablespoons wine vinegar, ½ teaspoon salt, freshly ground black pepper to taste, and 2 teaspoons dry mustard. Stirring, in the French manner, with the flat of a fork, add gradually 6 tablespoons peanut oil (French if available) until the dressing is homogenized. Add 1 tablespoon chopped parsley. Tear Boston lettuce into bite-size pieces and toss with the dressing. Arrange lengths of Belgian endive over lettuce sun-burst fashion, with tops of leaves pointing out. Serves 4.

Pear Fruit Cup: Combine 2 cups cut orange segments or cantaloupe balls, 2 fresh peeled and diced Bartlett pears,

1 cup stemmed seedless white grapes, and 4 fresh mint leaves in a bowl. Mix ½ cup orange juice with 2 tablespoons sugar. Pour over mixed fruits. Divide into 4 sherbet dishes or fruit bowls. Top each serving with a mint leaf. Serves 4.

Coffee

CHEESE FONDUE, Geneva-style

    2 canned truffles, or ½ cup mushrooms with liquid
    2 cups brut champagne
    1 pound aged Swiss cheese, coarsely grated
    2 tablespoons flour
    2 egg yolks
      White pepper

PART I   (IN ADVANCE):

Slice truffles, or mushrooms and reserve liquid. In a fondue pot, over medium heat, warm truffles or mushrooms in 1⅔ cups champagne. Toss grated cheese with flour. Turn heat to low. Add the cheese mixture, ⅓ at a time, to the fondue pot and stir until blended and smooth. Keep heat low. Beat egg yolks with the truffle or mushroom liquid and the remaining ⅓ cup of champagne. Add a dusting of white pepper. Slowly add the mixture to the cheese fondue and heat thoroughly, but do not allow fondue to boil.

(*Note:* For blender preparation, see page 20, step 9. Do not process sliced truffles or mushrooms in blender, merely stir into heated fondue mixture.)

PART II   (FONDUE POT OVER TABLE BURNER;
USE MEDIUM SETTING ON ELECTRIC FONDUE):

Adjust burner (placed on tray or mat) so that the fondue simmers throughout the meal. Fill a basket with crusty bread cubes and provide each guest with a plate and a fondue fork. Then pass the basket and the fondue fun begins.

PART III (EACH GUEST):

Spears bread cubes on his fondue fork through soft side of crust and then dunks it into the pot, giving a good stir each time. Serves 4.

3. FONDUE WITH MIXED CHEESES

The fondue menu, and the actual components of the fondue itself, have come a crooked mountain-mile since the legendary shepherd melted his coarse mountain cheese in that iron pot. Although modern interpretations of the classic fondue are still simple to prepare, they are enhanced and perfected through the use of additional ingredients and, above all, of specialty cheeses. For a delicious fondue, try a combination such as Emmentaler, Gruyère and Appenzeller, always remembering that you must use *natural, as opposed to processed,* and properly aged top-quality cheeses, both for cooking and flavoring, if the results are to meet with your legitimate expectations. A specialty-cheese fondue forms the not-hard-at-all core of a repast that would do any hostess proud, sparked by a good German Moselle, a salad, and an elegant dessert.

A parenthetical word about crust. Towards the end of the meal (and this applies to all cheese fondues) the cheese gets crusty at the bottom of the pot. This crust is considered, and rightly so, a delicacy in Switzerland. Tell your fondue-funmates to stir brisky, but *not clear to the bottom,* or no crust will form, and you'll miss out on one of the niceties of the whole shebang. Once the liquid's been consumed, divide and serve that bottom crust-formation to the lucky gluttons on hand.

MENU

Cheese Fondue, Specialty Cheeses—recipe follows
Cubes of Italian or French Bread
Wine: Moselle or Kirsch

Grüner Salat (Green Salad): Wash 1 head Boston lettuce and 2 heads chicory. Drain them and wrap in paper toweling. Crisp in the refrigerator. Tear into bite-size pieces and place in salad bowl with 1 tablespoon chopped parsley. Mix 3 tablespoons salad oil, 2 tablespoons cider vinegar, 1 teaspoon sugar, salt and pepper to taste. Pour over salad. Toss leaves well and let stand for 15 minutes before serving. Serves 6. *Note:* Host may prepare salad at table, provided salad greens are placed in bowl ahead of time.

Rote Grutze (Red Pudding): Wash 1 cup raspberries, 1 cup red currants, and 1 cup dark bing cherries and pit cherries. Cook with ½ cup water and ¾ cup granulated sugar for 5 to 6 minutes, or until tender. Blend ¼ cup cornstarch with the water and stir into the fruit mixture, stirring until smooth, and continue to cook until clear and thickened. Chill until ready to serve. Use as a filling for 6 meringue shells.

Meringue Shells (for Rote Grutze): Add dash salt, ½ teaspoon vinegar, and ¼ teaspoon vanilla to 3 egg whites; beat until mixture forms peaks. Add 1 cup sugar gradually; continue beating till very stiff. Spoon into 6 large mounds on cooky sheet covered with plain ungreased paper; shape cups with spoon. Bake in slow oven (300°F.) for 45 minutes. Remove from paper immediately. Cool. Serves 6.

Coffee

CHEESE FONDUE, Specialty Cheeses

2 cups Moselle wine
1 clove fresh garlic
6 ounces Emmentaler, grated or minced
½ pound Gruyère, grated or minced
4 ounces Appenzeller, grated or minced (if not available use
    more of the other cheeses)
1 tablespoon cornstarch
¼ cup kirsch
2 tablespoons butter
  Salt and pepper, to taste
  Freshly ground nutmeg, to taste, approximately ¼ teaspoon

PART I (IN ADVANCE):

Heat wine with the garlic in the fondue pot, using moderate heat, until wine reduces slightly (about 15 minutes). Then discard the garlic and add cheese by handfuls, ⅓ at a time, stirring constantly with a wooden fork or spoon until cheese is melted. Mix cornstarch with kirsch. Bring fondue to a bubble briefly (a few seconds) and add the cornstarch and kirsch and butter. Season lightly with the salt, pepper and nutmeg, stirring until blended.

(*Note:* For blender preparation, see page 20, step 9. Reduce garlic to ½ clove.

PART II (FONDUE POT OVER TABLE BURNER;
USE MEDIUM SETTING ON ELECTRIC FONDUE):

Adjust the burner so that the fondue will simmer slowly throughout the meal. If fondue becomes too thick, add heated wine, a bit at a time, and stir briskly.

PART III (EACH GUEST):

Spears a cube of bread through the soft side of crust and then dunks it into the pot, giving a good stir each time. Serves 6 as a main dish and 14-16 as appetizer.

4. FONTINA: THE BABY FONDUE

Fontina is called the baby, or milk, fondue because it contains no liquor, but extra filip can be given it with the addition of caraway seeds. In the canton of Valais, it's served fondue-fashion, bubbling in a pot right at the table, guests dunking their speared bread cubes into the pot as described above. I urge you, if you can come by it, to serve Merlot (mare-low), a refreshing dry red Swiss wine, at room temperature; a good red Bordeaux is a more-than-acceptable substitute. (See more on Fontina cheese as used in the superb Piedmont Fonduta, in the upcoming chapter on Italy.)

A mini-sized addendum on fontina: it's never too early to initiate the miniset into the fun of fondue. Liquorless fontina's the ideal choice. Use it as the stellar party attraction on a moppet-menu by omitting the wine and the fruit baked in wine-sauce listed below; substitute jello or fresh fruit in quantity, have rows of grapejuice or cola-drink bottles on tap, turn up the phonograph and turn the kids loose with an easy conscience.

MENU

Cheese Fondue, Fontina—recipe follows
Cubes of Italian or French Bread
Wine: Merlot or Red Bordeaux
Cold Stuffed Tomatoes: (Can be prepared well in advance.) Choose 4 firm, ripe tomatoes as nearly the same size as possible. Cut a slice from the top of each, carefully scoop out the pulp, season the shells with salt and pepper, and turn them upside-down on paper toweling to drain. Mix 1½ tablespoons olive oil and 1½ teaspoons lemon juice and use a pastry brush to coat the insides of the tomatoes with the dressing. Chill. Mix 2 cups cooked peas, well-drained and seasoned with salt and pepper, with just enough mayonnaise to moisten, chill well and then fill hollowed-out tomato shells. Garnish with a sprig of parsley or mint. Serves 4.

Fruit Baked in Wine Sauce: Thoroughly mix or blend in blender 1 cup light corn syrup and 1 cup Merlot, Bordeaux, or any other dry red wine you are serving. Put 2 Bartlett pears, peeled, cored and cut in half, 2 apples, peeled, cored and quartered, and 1 cup of seedless grapes in a baking dish, sprinkle with 6 whole cloves, ½ teaspoon coriander seeds, pinch of salt, and 6 allspice berries, and place a cinnamon stick on top. Cover with the wine-syrup mixture. Arrange a lemon quarter cut in thin slices over top. Bake in a moderate oven (350°F.) about 45 minutes, or until the fruit is soft and transparent. Baste every 20 minutes to keep fruit from becoming dry. Serves 4-6. *Note:* 5 fresh peaches may be substituted for the apple, pear and grape combination.

Coffee

CHEESE FONDUE, FONTINA

  1 teaspoon caraway seeds
  ¼ cup hot water
  2 tablespoons butter
  3 tablespoons flour
2½ cups milk
  1 pound Emmantaler, grated or minced
  1 teaspoon salt
    Pinch of nutmeg

PART I   (IN ADVANCE):

Soak caraway seeds in hot water for 15 minutes. Melt butter in fondue pot over low heat, add flour to make a roux, gradually add the milk and continue to cook over low heat until mixture becomes thick and smooth. Add the well-drained caraway seeds and again bring mixture to a simmer. Add cheese by handfuls, ⅓ at a time, stirring constantly with a wooden fork or spoon until cheese is melted. Bring fondue to a bubble briefly (a few seconds). Add the salt and nutmeg, stirring until blended.

Note: For blender preparation, see Chapter I, Fondue Cookery Clues: Cheese, Step 9. Do not process caraway seeds in blender, merely stir into heated fondue mixture.

PART II   (FONDUE POT OVER TABLE BURNER;
USE MEDIUM SETTING ON ELECTRIC FONDUE):

Adjust the burner so that the fondue will simmer slowly throughout the meal. If fondue should separate, combine ½ teaspoon cornstarch with one tablespoon of water or milk and stir into the fondue.

PART III   (EACH GUEST):

Spears a cube of bread through soft side of crust and then dunks it into the pot, giving a good stir each time.

Towards the end of the meal the cheese gets crusty at the bottom of the fondue pot. The crust is considered a delicacy and should be evenly divided among the diners. Serves 4 as a main dish or 10-12 as an appetizer.

5. RACLETTE AND YOUR OWN SWISS NEW YEAR'S PARTY.

In Switzerland, the New Year's festivities are like those in other parts of the world, only somewhat more so. Merrymaking and rounds of calls are the order of the day, and the menu I'm proposing, featuring the Raclette cheese fondue, may well be your authentic and informal solution to giving a New Year's party that's at once distinctive and ideally suited to the spirit and customs of the occasion.

Raclette is the name applied to a typical Swiss dish and also to a cheese, both originally from the canton of Valais, but obtainable in most parts of Switzerland (dish *and* cheese) and in a few restaurants in New York City. Its name is derived from the French verb *racler*, to scrape—see why below. The cheese, like its nearest-of-kin Gruyère and Emmentaler, is made in wheels, but weighs, per wheel, only about 15 pounds. (Don't panic; it can be ordered in half-wheels too.) It is firm-textured, naturally aged, and has a mild but unique flavor when served hot: in short, a perfect cheese for this use. Any surplus Raclette will be subsequently serviceable with macaroni or potato dishes. You'll note that the appropriate New Year's beverage is a variant from other fondue potables discussed in this chapter: Krambambuli (no Swisser name exists!) is a flaming wine-rum punch. It's served in a punch bowl, and when you ignite it and turn out the lights, the magic begins. (Details to follow, see "Krambambuli" below.)

Because you're dealing with a wheel, or half-wheel (this

could be called the wheeler-dealer fondue), the preparation of Raclette is quite a diverting sport in itself. Depending on your equipment, you may use, for heating, not the earlier-mentioned stove-top, but a wood-burning fire. It's said that the firewood permeates the fatty cheese as it hisses and bubbles in front of the flames. Lacking a fireplace, or electric heater, you can cut the Raclette in thin slices from the wheel, place it on flameproof plates, and broil it in the oven as you would a steak. The cheese will be melted and bubbling in approximately two minutes.

Although Raclette is not a dunking dish in the fondue sense of the word, it *is* melted, and the gathering-round the table spirit is the same.

MENU

Krambambuli (Flaming Wine-Rum Punch): Heat 2 bottles light, dry red wine in flameproof punch bowl placed over fondue burner. Do not boil wine as this will kill the flavor. Add ¾ cup lemon juice, ⅔ cup orange juice and 1 teaspoon cinnamon. Meanwhile slightly warm 1¼ cups Coruba or Meyer's rum in a separate pan. Now place 1 sugar loaf or 2½ cups cubed sugar on ladle or strainer; rest across top of punch bowl. Ladle warmed rum care-

fully over the sugar and ignite. Lights out! The magic begins. Blue flames dance around the sugar and melt it into the punch bowl. When the fire burns low add more rum. With the last drops of rum the sugar should have melted. Stir well and serve in heat-resistant glasses to your expectant guests. Pass around salted mixed nuts with this festive drink. Krambambuli lingers long on the palate and in the memory. Serves 6.

Mixed Salted Nuts

Cheese Fondue, Raclette—recipe follows

Holiday Cookies: Basler Brünsli. Beat 2 egg whites until foamy, gradually add 1 cup sugar and continue beating until egg whites stand in stiff peaks. Lightly mix 1 cup finely ground almonds, 2 ounces of grated unsweetened baking chocolate, 1 teaspoon cinnamon, and ¼ teaspoon ground cloves. Gently fold mixture into the beaten egg whites. Then add 3 tablespoons kirsch. Drop the mixture onto well-greased baking sheet and bake in a moderate oven (350°F.) for 10-12 minutes. Cookies should be soft on the inside. Makes 3 dozen cookies.

Mailänderli. Cream together 5 tablespoons butter and 5 tablespoons sugar, add 2 beaten eggs, ¼ teaspoon salt and grated peel of 1 lemon. Blend thoroughly. Sift 1¼ cups sifted flour with 1 teaspoon baking powder; gradually add to the creamed mixture. Cover the dough with a cloth and let it stand for 30 minutes. Roll out on a floured board to ½-inch thickness, cut into small cookies with a cutter. Brush tops with lightly beaten egg yolk and bake on a well-greased baking sheet in a moderate oven (350°F.) for 10-12 minutes or until light golden. Tradition says they must not be baked too long. Makes 2 dozen cookies.

Coffee

CHEESE FONDUE (Raclette)

½ wheel (7½ pounds) Raclette cheese (see Source of Supply)
  Freshly ground pepper and nutmeg
12 potatoes boiled in jackets
  Small bowls of pearl onions
  Small bowls of small green pickles

The preparation of raclette can be quite informal and very amusing, especially since the procedure begins with the half-wheel of cheese. Ideally, as stated above, raclette is prepared in front of a woodburning fire; it can also be made by placing the half-wheel of cheese in front of an electric heater.

The fun begins with a mitt and wide tongs for holding the half-wheel of cheese; bricks or a fireproof base (a broiler pan will do) for resting the cheese, and a scraper (*raclette!*) or large knife. Place the cut side of the wheel of cheese to face the fire or electric heater. When the surface begins to melt, each guest puts on the mitt and in turn scrapes the melted part of the cheese onto his plate, to be eaten with bites of boiled potatoes, onions and green pickles. Fresh pepper corns or nutmeg may be ground onto the raclette. Plates must be kept as warm as possible to prevent the raclette from hardening. Serves 6.

6. ENTER BEEF: FONDUE BOURGUIGNONNE.

Time for another "origin" legend; this one's also a product of Swiss lore, but the scene shifts from Alpine peaks to the famous vineyards of Burgundy, which lightly touch the border between France and Switzerland. When the precious world-famous grapes of this area ripen, they must be picked immediately, and, in days of yore, so goes the Swiss legend, the pickers couldn't take time out to eat until the pickings were completed. Necessity, acting upon some ingenious soul in extremity, always proves to be the mother of invention; in this case, the invention of the beef fondue: a certain harvester, frantic with hunger while picking furiously, stopped long enough to heat up a pot of boiling oil, and, dunk-cooking small hunks of meat in his spare moments, he ate on the run. Pick, dunk; pick, dunk—so neither the urgencies of the harvest nor his appetite suffered. The idea, like all inherently good ones, caught on fast: soon each picker was bringing his own meat to the communal oil-pot and cooking it to his own taste, while simultaneously stripping the vines of their juice-laden fruits. Thus, claim the Swiss, beef fondue, naturally called Fondue Bourguignonne, had its beginnings.

And beef fondue, made with beef cubes dipped in boiling oil, accompanied by an appetizing variety of sauces, made its appearance in the high-altitude Swiss villages in the 1950's, thanks, as earlier described, to the emergence of local prosperity when Alpine skiing became a magnet for the international set. Fondue of beef is a great after-skiing dish, especially since it can be made in a very short time. There are other less obvious advantages accruing to the thrifty, enterprising Swiss innkeepers who run the elaborate ski lodges. Can it be that they've added to their tidy fortunes by permitting the guests to do their own cooking, in the name of rare fun and gourmet gourmandise? Surely you remember how Tom Sawyer managed to get his fence painted!

In any case, "Fondue Bourguignonne" (boor'-guee-n'yonn) as applied to the Swiss version is, strictly speaking, a misnomer: it neither uses red wine (Burgundy) nor is it listed as a dish in the Burgundy provincial glossary of

French foods. But it was the fondue-loving Swiss who developed the entertaining ritual into the classic form, and the fun-loving ski enthusiasts who took the Fun-Fondue party idea back to their native lands to initiate an entirely new concept of informal entertaining.

Strictly speaking, I should label this portion of my Swiss chapter "Austria"; it was in 1963 that I encountered Fondu Bourguignonne, head-on, in the course of a trip to Salzburg to visit mutual friends who were studying at the Salzburg Seminar in American Studies.

My friends were living in the elegant former home of Max Reinhardt, located in Leopoldskron, just a short distance down the road from the Villa Trapp, the original home of the Trapp Family Singers. The Reinhardt Villa had been converted by the Seminar into dormitory-style quarters for students; entertainment space was, accordingly, limited, and my thoughtful friends had made arrangements for me to stay at the Pension Nonntal, Waschergasse 7 und 9, in Salzburg. The Nonntal is the kind of inn one frequently encounters in Bavaria, full of charm, enchantment and tradition, situated at one of Salzburg's most beautiful vantage-points, offering a background view of the fortress Hohensalzburg and the ever-lovely Bavarian Alps.

This, then, was the setting for my introduction to Fondue Bourguignonne. Frau Fenninger, the wife of the owner, conducted us through the establishment, told us that the decorating of the cozy cafe-dining room had been her personal pet project, and that, if we would dine there that evening, she would privately prepare for us the specialty of the house. Reservations were made for four.

The dinner hour in Austria is from 6 to 9; in Salzburg,

particularly, it's wisest to book meals in your own hotel, as the tourist season flourishes the year round, and hotel dining rooms always serve their own guests first. In any case, we had no problem at the Nonntal: Frau Fenninger had set up our four-person Fondue Bourguignonne table in the manner of a true artist. A stewardess friend who had accompanied me on my Salzburg jaunt was so overwhelmed by the attractive simplicity of the fondue table appointments that she immediately started making sketches of plans to convert her own New York apartment dining alcove into a small reproduction of the Cafe Nonntal, and has made fun fondue parties her entertaining specialty ever since. For us, Fondue Bourguignonne will always be Frau Fenninger, Salzburg, and the Pension Nonntal.

Before launching into the menu and recipes, a word about the beverage: Austrian wines are considered superlative—by the Austrians in any case. "Ein Viertel," which is ½ liter or about ½ pint, is very inexpensive. But bottled, vintage wines are costly, and are very hard to come by in the United States. So my own choice with Fondue Bourguignonne is either a good Burgundy or, of all things, Spanish sangría, a heady, infinitely variable wine-cum-fruit-and-other ingredients mixture, of which two versions follow.

MENU

Fondue Bourguignonne—recipe follows
Six Sauces for Fondue Bourguignonne—recipes follow
Roesti (Swiss-style browned potatoes): Cook 1½ pounds potatoes in their skins and peel when cold; grate coarsely. Heat a skillet with butter. Add grated potatoes and season to taste with salt and pepper. Turn potatoes with a spatula to brown all over. Add more butter if neces-

sary. Finally, flatten potatoes into a pancake and brown on each side, about 20-30 minutes. Serves 6.

Green Salad with Sauce Vinaigrette: To mix a green salad for 6, wash lettuce, drain well, wrap in paper toweling and refrigerate to crisp. Rub a large bowl lightly with a cut clove of garlic. Put in chilled greens (Boston lettuce, romaine and escarole), tearing large leaves into small pieces. Then add Sauce Vinaigrette, a little at a time, tossing greens lightly to coat all leaves well.

Sauce Vinaigrette: Combine 1 cup peanut oil, ⅓ cup tarragon vinegar, ½ teaspoon salt, ¼ teaspoon freshly-ground black pepper, ¼ teaspoon sugar and 1 teaspoon Dijon mustard in a bowl. Beat until well blended. Stir in 2 teaspoons minced shallots or onions, 2 tablespoons minced parsley and 1 clove finely minced garlic. Let stand at room temperature for 30 minutes to allow flavors to blend. Stir Sauce Vinaigrette just before mixing with the salad greens. Makes 1½ cups. *Note:* I detest sweet salad dressings but the ¼ teaspoon sugar does no more than counteract some of the acidity. Do try it.

Wine: Sangría or Burgundy. Sangría I. Boil ½ cup water and 1 cup sugar with ¼ teaspoon cinnamon for 5 minutes and let syrup cool. Combine 1 unpeeled lemon cut into slices, 2 bananas peeled and cut into thick slices and 1 peeled orange cut into thick slices; now cover the fruit with the cooled syrup. Chill the fruit mixture for several hours. Put ice cubes in a 2-quart pitcher and add the chilled ingredients, then stir in 1 quart medium-dry red wine. Stir the mixture thoroughly, mashing the fruit slightly. Serve the Sangría in well-chilled tumblers, garnishing each glass with some of the sliced fruit. (Less potent than II and therefore more suitable for a fondue luncheon.) Serves 6.

Sangría II. Mix ⅓ cup orange juice, 3 tablespoon lemon juice and 2 tablespoons confectioners' sugar in large (2½-quart) pitcher. Mix in 4 ounces brandy, 4 ounces orange Cointreau and 8 ice cubes. Add 1 quart red wine and 1 cup club soda. Stir well. Pour into well-chilled tumblers, garnishing each with an orange and lemon slice. Serves 6.

Cheese: Emmentaler-Edam-Mondseer (see Source of Supply)

Fruit Bowl

Alternate Desserts: Pêches Flambées. Dissolve 1 cup sugar in 1½ cups water, bring to a boil and cook it for 10 minutes. Add 6 peeled peaches (halved) and simmer for about 5 minutes, or until fruit is just tender. Remove the peaches and syrup to a flambé skillet and place over blazer or fondue burner. Keep the heat high. Bring the syrup again to a boil. Pour over the peaches ¼ cup warmed Armagnac brandy and ignite the spirit. Serves 6.

Salzburger Nockerln (as prepared at St. Peter Stiftkeller in Salzburg). Cream ½ cup butter and ¼ cup sugar; gradually add and blend in 3 lightly beaten egg yolks. Fold in stiffly beaten egg whites. Dust top with 1 tablespoon flour and blend well. Pour 3 tablespoons melted butter into 9- or 10-inch frying pan and add the batter. Set on an asbestos mat over low heat for 3-4 minutes until the bottom of the batter starts to turn a light golden. Then cut the nockerln with a tablespoon and turn each piece to continue cooking. They should be light golden all over; do not let them brown. Serve immediately, sprinkle with confectioners' sugar. Do not let them stand, they "wither." Serves 6.

FONDUE BOURGUIGNONNE, (Basic Recipe)

3 pounds prime beefsteak (sirloin, fillet or shell)
   cut into 1-inch cubes
   Salt and pepper to taste
   Peanut or corn oil, approximately 3 cups
   Assorted Sauces

PART I   (IN ADVANCE):

Let meat stand at room temperature for 30 minutes. Blot
excess moisture with paper toweling. Lightly salt and pepper the meat. Arrange on wooden or china platters and
garnish with parsley or watercress. Fill the fondue pot ½
full of peanut or corn oil. (Olive oil has too penetrating a
taste and butter will burn unless it is clarified.) Heat to
about 375°F. on a deep fat thermometer. (Use highest setting on electric fondue.) If you have no thermometer, test
fat with a small bread cube. Oil is hot enough when it
cooks the bread brown and crisp in 30-40 seconds.

PART II   (FONDUE POT OVER TABLE BURNER;
USE HIGHEST SETTING ON ELECTRIC FONDUE):

To protect the table top, place tray under table burner.
Adjust burner so that oil remains at proper temperature
throughout the meal.

PART III   (EACH GUEST):

First helps himself to the sauces and other accompani-
ments, which he puts on his serving plate. He then spears
a cube of meat with the fondue fork or skewer and dunks
it into the hot fat, cooking it to his taste—10-20 seconds for
rare and 50-60 seconds for well-done. The fondue fork or
skewer will be very hot; therefore, the guest transfers meat
to a dinner fork, and dips it in the sauce of his choice.

The first fork or skewer will have cooled sufficiently by this time, and the guest can start another piece of meat cooking. Usually 3 people can cook their meat at the same time. More than this number may cause the temperature of the oil to overcool unless you are using an electric fondue pot. Serves 6.

* *Note:* To clarify butter melt over low heat. When it is completely melted remove from the stove burner. Allow the solids to settle to the bottom of the pan. Strain the butter through a very fine sieve or muslin cloth into a jar. This is clarified butter, and is now ready to use in the fondue pot, to replace an equal amount of oil.

SIX SAUCES FOR
FONDUE BOURGUIGNONNE

An inventive hostess will enjoy the fun of creating her own selection of sauces, to be passed around at the table. Keep in mind the flavor and color combinations, since the sauces can be arranged around the fondue burner attractively enough to create a centerpiece.

The blender is used for all the sauces. In fact, this electric appliance has done for gourmet cooking what the wheel has done for transportation!

HORSERADISH SAUCE

    ½ cup mayonnaise
    ¼ cup dairy sour cream
    2 tablespoons grated horseradish
    Salt to taste

GREEN SAUCE

   1 egg
   ½ cup olive oil
   ¼ cup white wine vinegar
   6 sprigs watercress (without long stems)
   1 teaspoon dried chervil
   ¼ cup fresh parsley
   2 tablespoons chives
   1 teaspoon salt
   ½ teaspoon pepper

CURRY SAUCE

   ½ cup mayonnaise
   ½ teaspoon sweet paprika
   1 teaspoon curry powder

SAUCE SUZEE, a New Orleans Remoulade Sauce.

   Blend the following for 30 seconds:
   ½ cup salad oil
   ½ cup olive oil
   ½ cup fresh horseradish, grated
   1 teaspoon white vinegar
   ¼ cup lemon juice
   2 tablespoons Worcestershire sauce
   ¼ cup Creole mustard, or Grey Poupon prepared Dijon mustard
   Then add the following:
   ¼ cup chopped green onion (scallions)
   ¼ cup chopped celery
   2 teaspoons chopped parsley
   ¼ cup paprika
   1 teaspoon whole cloves
   1 teaspoon chopped dried bay leaves
   1 clove garlic
   ½ teaspoon dried thyme
   1½ teaspoons salt
      Pinch of black and red pepper
      "21" Club Sauce Maison, optional (see Sources of Supply)
   Blend another 30 seconds, or until thoroughly puréed.

ANCHOVY BUTTER

    1 two-ounce can anchovy fillets
    ⅓ cup butter, softened
    2 tablespoons olive oil
    ⅛ teaspoon freshly-ground pepper

MAJOR GREY'S CHUTNEY (to be purchased)

7. GERMAN ANCESTRY: BEEF FONDUE WITH SAUCES.

Not all of my fondue finds are the well-earned fruits of my own peregrinations. I hereby confess that the recipe for Fondue Bacchus was left in my company mailbox by a mysterious stewardess who must forever remain anonymous, as she neglected to sign her name. Her immortality is assured, however, by this second of our beef fondue recipes.

As to its area of origin, I can deduce only from the ingredients of the recipe. The choice of wines would indicate that is was dreamed up by the inhabitants of that hybrid region lying close to the German-French border, near Strasbourg, home of the famed pâté de foie gras. This, the northernmost wine-growing area of Europe, produces the delicate Moselle, Rhine and Alsatian white wines; properly speaking, then, it's a German-Alsatian fondue that's filtered its way down into the French-German sector of Switzerland, so I'm including it in the Swiss section of our book. The court bouillon used to cook the meat is typically French; the notion of serving the bouillon together with thin slices of buttered pumpernickel as a soup course, following the fondue itself, is typically German. I consider this recipe one of the really unusual topnotchers of my entire fondue collection.

MENU

Spirited Chicken Liver Pâté: Heat ¾ cup butter over low heat; add 4 medium onions, finely chopped, and sauté slowly until onions are golden but not brown. Add 1½ pounds chicken livers and 1 cup dry sherry; cover and cook over low heat 30 minutes. Cool. Stir in 6 tablespoons brandy, 1½ teaspoons salt, and freshly ground pepper to taste. Puree in electric blender until smooth, or put through food mill or sieve. Put into buttered 4-cup mold, or small individual casseroles, and chill thoroughly. Serve unmolded with saltines or Melba toast rounds. Note: It is important to add the brandy and seasoning after cooking. "Sherry to cook, brandy to finish" is the cooking rule.

Fondue Bacchus—recipe follows

German Sauces for Fondue Bacchus—recipes follow

Wine: Moselle, Rhine or Alsatian

Fondue Broth with Thin Slices of Pumpernickel

Butter

Colorful Spinach Salad: Wash and pick over ½ pound fresh young spinach leaves. Remove the stems and drain well. Wrap in paper toweling and refrigerate until needed. In a large salad bowl combine the spinach, ½ large cucumber (peeled and sliced in thin rounds), 1 green pepper and 1 red pepper cut in strips, 1 red apple unpeeled and diced, 3 small carrots sliced in thin rounds, and 2 medium-size tomatoes cut in wedges. Blend ½ teaspoon salt, freshly-ground black pepper to taste, ¼ cup white vinegar, 4 tablespoons olive oil, 1 tablespoon sugar, 3 tablespoons yogurt and 1 tablespoon fresh dill (or 1 teaspoon dried). Pour over the salad mixture and toss until well mixed. Garnish with hard-cooked egg and chopped chives. Serve at once. Serves 6.

Bombe Cardinal: Thaw out 1 package (12-ounce) of frozen peach slices but do not drain them. Combine the peaches, ½ cup French grenadine syrup (*sirop de grenadine*—see Source of Supply), 1 cup commercial sour cream and 1 quart vanilla ice cream in a large bowl, and beat with an electric mixer or rotary eggbeater until smooth and well-blended. Pour mixture into a 2-quart mold, or individual molds. Freeze until firm. Unmold by dipping into lukewarm water for a few seconds. Garnish with crystallized violets and mint leaves. Serves 6.

FONDUE BACCHUS

> 2 cups strong chicken broth
> 2 cups white wine (Moselle, Rhine or Alsatian)
> 1 medium onion, thinly sliced
> 3 ribs of celery with leaves, chopped
> 1 fresh garlic clove, chopped
> 8 juniper berries, crushed
> 10 peppercorns, crushed
> ½ teaspoon salt, or to taste
> 1 tablespoon chopped fresh tarragon leaves or
>   1 teaspoon of dried
> 2 sprigs fresh thyme or ½ teaspoon of dried
> 2 sprigs parsley
> 1 bay leaf
> 3 pounds prime beefsteak (sirloin, fillet or shell)
>   cut into 1-inch cubes
> Assorted sauces

PART I   (IN ADVANCE):

Three days before serving, heat chicken broth and wine to boiling. Add the onion, celery, garlic, juniper berries, peppercorns, salt, tarragon, thyme, parsley and bay leaf.

Bring to boil again. Cool and then refrigerate until party time.

Strain the broth mixture through a fine sieve and pour into fondue pot. Bring to a boil.

Note: Blender method; no pre-chopping necessary. Three days before serving, heat chicken broth and 1 cup of wine to boiling in large saucepan. Meanwhile, put remaining cup of wine and all other ingredients except meat into blender container, cover and process until finely chopped. Add to boiling broth-wine mixture and bring to a boil again. Cool and refrigerate until party time. When ready to serve, strain the broth mixture through a fine sieve and pour into fondue pot. Bring to a boil.

PART II   (FONDUE POT OVER TABLE BURNER;
USE MEDIUM SETTING ON ELECTRIC FONDUE) :

To protect the table top, place tray under table burner. Adjust burner so that broth will boil throughout the meal.

PART III   (EACH GUEST) :

First helps himself to the sauces, which he puts on his serving plate. He then spears a cube of meat with the fondue fork or skewer and dunks it into the boiling broth, cooking it to his taste—10 to 20 seconds for rare and 50 to 60 seconds for well-done. The fondue fork or skewer will be very hot; therefore, the guest should transfer his meat to a second fork to dip in the sauce of his choice. The first fork or skewer will have cooled sufficiently by this time, and the guest can start another piece of meat cooking. Usually 3 to 4 people can cook their meat at the same time. Serves 6. *Note:* The broth is now served as a separate course, with thin slices of pumpernickel.

GERMAN SAUCES (FONDUE BACCHUS)

HOT GINGER SAUCE:

    2 tablespoons butter
    2 tablespoons flour
    ¾ cup water
    ¾ cup white wine
    2 tablespoons white wine vinegar
    ½ cup raisins, chopped
    3 tablespoons brown sugar
    1 lemon (juice and rind)
    ½ cup candied ginger, finely chopped
       Pinch of ginger powder

Melt butter in heavy saucepan, add flour and blend. Add the water and wine, stirring constantly. Add vinegar, raisins, brown sugar, lemon juice and grated rind, candied ginger and ginger powder. Cook 15 minutes, stirring constantly. Makes approximately 2 cups. In Germany, hot ginger sauce is often served with cold tongue.

Note: Blender method; no pre-chopping necessary. Melt butter in heavy saucepan. Put remaining ingredients into blender container, cover and process until raisins and ginger are finely chopped. Add to saucepan, mix well with butter and cook over medium heat about 15 minutes stirring constantly.

GYPSY SAUCE:

    ¾ cup mayonnaise
    ¼ cup yogurt
    ¼ teaspoon dry mustard
    1 teaspoon capers, chopped
    2 small sweet gherkins, finely chopped
    1 small onion, grated
    1 hard-cooked egg, finely chopped
    1 teaspoon chives, chopped
    1 teaspoon parsley, chopped
       Salt and pepper to taste

Put ingredients into blender container, cover and process until ingredients are finely chopped.

SHARP TOMATO SAUCE:

    1 cup tomato catsup
    2 teaspoons prepared mustard
    2 tablespoons lemon juice
    1 medium onion, grated
    3 dashes of Tabasco
    3 tablespoons chili sauce
    1 tablespoon parsley, chopped
    ½ teaspoon dried tarragon
    3 dashes of garlic juice
        Salt and pepper to taste.

Purée ingredients in a blender or put ingredients in a 1-quart screw top jar and shake vigorously. Chill. Makes approximately 2 cups.

Germans love remoulade sauce. There are as many brands on the grocery shelves as we have of mayonnaise in this country. Use leftover sauce for cold seafood.

REMOULADE SAUCE:

    1 cup mayonnaise
    2 teaspoons fresh tarragon, chopped or ⅔ teaspoon of dried
    1 tablespoon parsley, chopped
    1 clove garlic (juice only)
    4 tablespoons sweet pickle relish
    1 tablespoon capers, finely chopped
    1 tablespoon lemon juice, or to taste
    2 tablespoons white wine vinegar
        White pepper and salt to taste

Put ingredients into blender container, cover and process until capers and parsley are finely chopped. Chill.

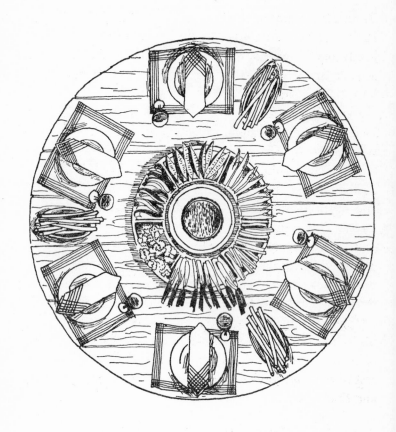

III ITALY: Fondues For La Dolce Vita

From Switzerland it's just a border-hop to the south into Italy, and as always, the border-crossing experience is a heady one: miraculously, within a few yards, it seems, accents, scenery, faces and architecture all change. And, let it be here stated, so do fondues.

Soon after we'd crossed the border into the northern Piedmont region of Italy, we stopped for lunch at a roadside *ristorante*. The establishment was typical of so many family-owned European restaurants: Papa is host, maître d', food-buyer, boss and sometimes chef as well; Mama and offspring do their stint in the kitchen and wait on tables. This typically Italian roadside inn was, like most such, a gathering-place where working-class folk could gossip while drinking their coffee from a complicated expresso urn, which, after much prolonged hissing and steaming, could finally be persuaded to produce a trickle of thick, syrupy liquid. Italian expresso coffee is roasted black, not brown, and is drunk either like café au lait, in 50-50 proportions with milk in the morning; or, during the rest of the day, served in demitasse form—no milk, strong, and thick.

8. BAGNA CAUDA, THE VEGETABLE SAUCEDIP.

It was at this first roadside luncheon stop that we became acquainted with our initial Italian version of fondue: bagna cauda. This is a hot vegetable saucedip, made with

anchovies, olive oil, butter, a soupçon of garlic, and sometimes a bit of cream. The bagna cauda is kept hot in small
earthenware pots which are set on curious little spirit
stoves placed between the seated guests. Breadsticks and
platters of raw vegetables are brought to the table, to be
dunked in the sauce. For liquid refreshment, one has a
choice of Barbera, Barolo, and Freisa, these being the
wines of the region, and considered some of the finest
vintages in Italy.

An informed fellow-traveler told me that in former
times, bagna cauda had been considered peasant fare in
the Piedmont, and was never included in tourist menus.
Meat is, of course, a luxury for the hardworking moun-
taineer of the region, and on those special occasions when
he does prepare a boiled beef, he uses the leftovers to dip
in the omnipresent bagna cauda.

We're already familiar with the cheese and beef versions of our subject; I now suggest that fondue, loosely
interpreted, can include an assortment of vegetables as
well, if they're given the fondue treatment. The cooking
technique for bagna cauda is so similar to that used for
other fondues that this Italian vegetable pot-pourri has
become a staple among my fondue party menus.

La bagna cauda makes a perfect light lunch; also, as it's
less weighty than the heftier fondues, it qualifies as a sub-
stantial cocktail repast before theatre: you won't fall asleep
on it, particularly if you quaff Italian expresso afterwards.
It can be refreshingly followed by such succulent fresh
fruit as yellow peaches and plump, juicy purple grapes;
these, incidentally, are lavishly nurtured by the marvelous
bracing climate of the Piedmont.

MENU

La Bagna Cauda—recipe follows

Hot Dip Sauce—recipe follows. Or use less oily sauces: Cheese Fondue Dipping Sauce, Mexican Dipping Sauce, or Hot Clam Curry Dipping Sauce; see Supplement for recipes.

Italian Breadsticks: The breadsticks of the Piedmont are made from the wheat of the region and are purely Turinese. They were a favorite of Napoleon, who referred to them as "those little Turinese sticks." However, they can be bought in any Italian bakery in the world and have long since lost their identity with Turin.

Wine: Barolo

Fruit: Purple Grapes and Peaches

Café Expresso

LA BAGNA CAUDA,
(Vegetables With Hot Dip)

> 1 large cucumber, peeled, seeded, and cut into
>   3-by-½-inch strips
> 3 carrots, peeled and cut into 3-by-½-inch strips
> 5 celery stalks, cut into 3-by-½-inch strips
> 1 green pepper, seeded and cut into 3-by-½-inch strips
> 2 bunches of Belgian endive, cut lengthwise into quarters
> 5 scallions, trimmed and cut into 3-inch lengths
> 1 small head of cauliflower, broken into separate flowers
>   Italian bread sticks
>   Cubes of roast or boiled beef, optional

Soak the prepared vegetable strips in a bowl of ice water for at least 1 hour to crisp them. Pat dry with paper towels, cover with plastic wrap and refrigerate.

HOT DIP SAUCE

¾ cup Italian olive oil
1 cup butter
1 teaspoon garlic, finely minced
8 flat anchovy fillets, drained, rinsed, and finely minced
¼ cup mushrooms, finely minced
1 tablespoon heavy cream, optional

PART I   (IN ADVANCE):

Heat the olive oil, butter and garlic in the fondue pot over low heat until the fat is melted. Add the anchovy fillets, mushrooms and (optional) heavy cream. Do not let the sauce boil, but keep warm for about 20 minutes in order to blend and mellow the flavors.

Note: Blender method; no pre-chopping necessary. Melt butter in fondue pot over medium heat. Put remaining ingredients except cream into blender container, cover and process until mushrooms are finely minced. Add to butter in fondue pot and add cream if desired. Keep warm over medium heat about 20 minutes before serving.

PART II   (FONDUE POT OVER TABLE BURNER;
USE MEDIUM SETTING ON ELECTRIC FONDUE):

About half an hour before the party, arrange vegetables on one large platter or two small ones. Flank with breadsticks in tall goblets. Adjust the burner so that dip stays fairly hot (but not boiling) throughout the meal.

PART III   (EACH GUEST):

Picks up a vegetable or breadstick with his fingers and dips it into the sauce. If beef is provided, provide settings of fondue forks or skewers as well. Serves 6.

9. FONDUTA: CHEESE AND TRUFFLES.

But the ubiquitous cheese fondue is found in Northern Italy as well. In the mountains of the Piedmont it's called Fonduta, and is made of Fontina cheese, which is melted to a whisper in egg yolks and perfumed with the special white truffles of the region. There are many who'll swear that the Fonduta of the Piedmont makes the Swiss fondue curdle by comparison.

(I'm told that an ideal gourmet's itinerary would recommend an October visit to the Piedmont to taste the Fonduta; it was late September when I was touring the region, but I can't imagine its tasting any better at any other time, ever.)

The Fontina cheese of the Piedmont is one of the fullest of Italian cheeses, somewhat superior to the version found in nearby Switzerland (see above). Whereas the Swiss Fontina is preferable as a table cheese, the Piedmontese claim, with some reason, that *their* Fontina is the only proper basis for the famous Fonduta dish. However, as I've indicated in the recipe that follows, some of us have substituted Gruyère (about which please see Cheese Glossary) without perceptibly disastrous results.

A word about truffles. The white variety found in the small town of Alba, not to be confused with the white truffles of North Africa, are said by some connoisseurs to be superior to the black truffles of France, for which the Perigord region is renowned. The truffle, in case you're a bit uncertain, is an unusual fungus related to the mushroom, but which grows underground, in the root-system of trees, at an altitude between 1,300 and 2,000 feet. [About the truffle versus the mushroom: the Italians claim that the truffle combined with cheese is so utterly right that no mere mushroom will do. However, W. M. Thackeray (no Italian he!) is reported to have said, "Mushrooms, thought I, are better than these tasteless truffles." Perhaps he never tasted *Italian* truffles, basing his negative judgment on the French. But anyhow, the controversy, for our purposes, is really academic: fresh white Italian truffles are unavailable in the United States. We'll suggest canned.]

Truffle-hunting is a highly refined technique, and the hunters work mostly at night, aided by dogs especially trained to sniff out the scent of the fungus. (Note: *French* truffles, for the record, are rooted out by pigs.) The hunters claim that the air is clearer at night and the truffle-scent more readily located by the dogs. That's one story; *I* was told that truffle-hunting takes place under cover of nocturnal secrecy so as to elude any watching poachers, since another truffle, and they really *are* delicious, will grow in the same spot. No trifling with truffles!

The Piedmontese, following the rule of French cuisine, combine the shaved truffle with the rich, subtle dishes of the region to produce their famous epicurean specialties. On the streets of Turin, chief city of the Piedmont region, you can see the truffle vendor with his shabby little black bag, peddling his prized booty from door to door of private homes and better restaurants.

As to these latter, Turin's fashionable Ristorante del Cambio is considered the finest in the region. A quick scanning of the menu will immediately dispel the popularly-held notion that Italian food is greasy, garlicky, and prepared with a tomato sauce base. The northern Piedmont borders France, and the cuisine is strongly influenced by the milk-and-butter culture of both countries. Here a tourist can dine in true elegance, starting with an aperitif of the famous white vermouth of Turin. (The Italians firmly believe that a drink of vermouth aids the digestion and, except for those who either fraternize with or wish to mimic Americans, they rarely drink pre-dinner cocktails.)

As the Fonduta menu will include antipasto, a word about that. The term, literally translated, means "before meal," and antipasto is, of course, the Italian version of hors-d'oeuvres. The Piedmontese components are customarily hard-cooked eggs in a variety of sauces, stuffed mushrooms, pickled artichokes, and such products as salami or or prosciutto.

A light broth (*not* minestrone) is likely to be served before the main course; other specialty goodies of the area are chestnuts coated in crystallized sugar ("marroni confetti"), toffees, biscuits, and other gourmet wickednesses.

Here, then, is a typical Piedmont dinner menu, featuring Fonduta, as it would be served in a deluxe restaurant in Turin:

MENU

Aperitif: White Vermouth

Antipasto: On a large serving platter, arrange marinated artichoke hearts, Italian-style mild Tuscan salad peppers, very hot pickled peppers, sweet red-pepper halves, ripe and stuffed green olives, paper-thin slices of pepperoni, salami roll-ups, and an assortment of Italian cheeses; also Eggs Anchovy.

Eggs Anchovy: Chill 6 hard-cooked eggs cut in half and scoop out yolks. Sieve egg yolks through a fine sieve, or use a blender. Chop 2 small tins of anchovy fillets and add to the egg yolk mixture. Add 1 tablespoon of vinegar and enough anchovy oil to make a smooth paste.

Season with salt and pepper to taste. Spoon the egg yolk mixture into a cake-defrosting bag with a star tip and stuff the egg white. Garnish with parsley or paprika. Serves 6.

Chicken Consommé

Fonduta with Triangles of Toasted Italian Bread—recipe follows

Rice: Melt 2 tablespoons of butter, add 1 clove of garlic and 1 sage leaf and sauté 3 minutes. Remove the garlic and sage leaf and pour the butter over 4 cups cooked rice. Salt to taste and heat thoroughly before serving. Serves 6.

Wine: Freisa Brut

Peaches Piedmont Style: Combine 6 macaroons which have been crushed, 6 tablespoons chopped salted almonds, 1 strip chopped candied orange peel, and 1 strip chopped candied lemon peel. Fill 6 peach halves with the mixture. Place another 6 halves on top of the filled halves to form the shape of a whole peach. Secure with toothpicks. Place on a shallow buttered baking dish. Pour 1 cup peach juice over the stuffed peaches and sprinkle with granulated sugar. Bake in a moderate oven (350°F.) until sugar forms a crust. About 20 minutes. Serve hot or cold.

FONDUTA

1 pound of imported Italian Fontina cheese, or Gruyère,
    minced or grated
1 teaspoon cornstarch dissolved in ½ cup milk
¼ teaspoon salt
⅛ teaspoon nutmeg
3 egg yolks
1 can Italian white truffles, sliced, or 1 cup raw mushrooms,
    sliced
6 slices Italian bread, toasted, buttered and cut in small triangles

PART I   (IN ADVANCE):

Combine cheese, cornstarch-milk mixture, salt and nutmeg in the fondue pot. Cook over low heat, stirring constantly, for about 5 minutes, or until the cheese melts; it will be somewhat stringy.

Beat the egg yolks in a bowl very lightly for a few seconds with a whisk. Spoon about ¼ cup of the hot cheese mixture into the yolks and beat them vigorously. Pour the mixture slowly back into the fondue pot, beating constantly, and continue cooking the cheese mixtures over low heat until it becomes smooth and finally begins to thicken to a heavy cream.

PART II   (FONDUE POT OVER TABLE BURNER;
USE MEDIUM SETTING ON ELECTRIC FONDUE):

Adjust the burner so that the fonduta will simmer slowly throughout the meal.

PART III   (EACH GUEST):

Ladles the fonduta over the toast triangles and sprinkles with the sliced truffles or mushrooms (or dips fondue fork, holding the toast triangles, into the fonduta). Serves 6.

10. A ROMAN FEAST AND FRITTO MISTO.

Stay off the beaten tourist track, I say; Rome, for me, will always be the Villa Eva, V.A.Morelli 1, a *pensione* in the heart of the city. It's so secluded that my taxi driver, unable to thread his way to the address I gave him, tried to talk me into staying at one of the large, glossy, characterless hotels catering to American tourists. (Sorry, but that's how most of them are.) Fortunately, I persisted in locating my quiet haven. After making inquiries of a convent and a policeman, we located the street number, hidden on a high wall and partially covered by hanging vines. I pushed my way through the foliage, clambered up several flights of rough stone steps, and found myself in one of the most charming spots in all of Rome. (If you've any similar leads, I urge you to stick with them: it's worth it.) The Villa had been the residence of an important Fascist general before the downfall of Mussolini had relieved him of his entertainment responsibilities; fortunately, vestiges of the former period have been maintained by the new owners, a couple from Hungary. (Many of Rome's most cherished pensions are, oddly enough, maintained by foreigners.)

Back to gastronomia: my arrival at the Villa Eva coincided with the lunch hour, and my initiation into fritto misto (fried mix). Before I list the Roman ingredients, be reassured: my American version will use a different set of basics. The Roman fritto misto is based on the popular and widely held Southern European theory that *any* cut of meat, however unlikely in its raw state, can be rendered palatable and appetizing by proper cooking and by blending with such highly persuasive ingredients as tomato, onion, garlic, peppers and herbs. So my Villa Eva misto consisted of three or four animal organs such as liver, sweetbreads, brains etc., cubed and cunningly disguised to mingle with raw vegetables dipped in batter, and fried in deep fat.

As I'm calling my fritto misto menu "A Roman Feast," and with good reason, a word about Roman cooking. Almost every type of regional food can be found in the ristorantes and trattorias of Rome, which cater in large part to the personal predilections of the proprietor and his (usually) amply proportioned wife rather than to the established tastes of the more elaborate tourist restaurants. This is why you'll find Veal Cutlets a la Marsala, which is a Sicilian wine, and Noodles alla Florentine legitimately adorning our Roman menu. I did learn that Roman cooking, although not, by and large, excessively refined or elaborate, is extremely savory. Use of animal fats, peppercorns, green peppers and aromatic herbs lend it piquancy and distinction. As to the wines, each course is customarily accompanied by the delectable vintage wines from the Alban Hills, the so-called Castelli wines, which combine a dry flavor with robust alcoholic content. The majority are of a golden amberlike color (Frascatti, Marino, Valetri), or with a russet or red tinge, as in those from Genzano. Wines tending toward sweetness include the white Cannelino of Frascati, and the red Aleatico of Piglio.

The following menu is a composite of all the good things served at the Villa Eva, including a clever, if non-Roman, way of preparing the fritto misto as a fondue course. I don't deny that this is a hearty menu, to put it mildly, but it does reflect the eating habits of the Romans. With just one exception, which admittedly bears an American accent: a traveler is more likely to find biscuit tortoni on a domestic menu than on the traditional Italian one. A pity, because the signora's version, given here below, is a delicious dessert, and easily prepared in advance.

MENU

Fritto Misto—recipe follows

Veal Cutlets Marsala: Place 12 slices of veal, scallopine-style, flat on a board; top each with a slice of boiled ham and a thin slice of mozzarella cheese. Fold in half and secure with toothpicks. In a heavy skillet heat ½ cup butter or Italian olive oil; add the veal rolls and cook until browned—approximately 20 minutes; remove to heated platter. To the brownings in the pan add ½ cup Marsala wine, ⅛ teaspoon salt, ⅛ teaspoon pepper and 1 teaspoon of butter; cook until heated—approximately 10 minutes. Pour over veal rolls and serve. Serves 6. This can be made ahead of time and reheated in low oven.

Noodles Alla Florentine: Sift 3¾ cups all-purpose flour, measure, and sift onto pastry board. Make a well in the center of the mound of flour. In it put ⅔ cup puréed spinach, 2 lightly beaten eggs, 3 tablespoons water, and ½ teaspoon salt. Then knead for 20 minutes. This will make a smooth, stiff, satiny dough. The long kneading is necessary to develop the elasticity of the dough. Roll the dough out to paper thinness. Divide the dough in smaller amounts for easier handling if necessary; then let it dry on boards or dishcloths if you do not have enough board space. When dry roll up jelly-roll fashion and cut into quarter-inch strips. Drop into a large kettle of boiling salted water to which a few drops of olive oil have been added. Cook until tender—about 12 minutes. Serves 6.

Italian Bread and Butter
Wine: Frascati
Italian Salad: Wash and drain 1 heart of escarole, 1 heart of endive, 1 head of romaine, and 1 heart of fennel. Wrap in paper toweling and crisp in the refrigerator along with 6 sliced radishes. Rub the salad bowl with 1 clove garlic. Mix ¾ cup Italian olive oil, 4 tablespoons wine vinegar, 1 tablespoon prepared mustard, 4 chopped anchovy fillets, ¼ teaspoon salt, and ¼ teaspoon freshly-ground black pepper. Place the salad greens and radishes in the salad bowl and drizzle the dressing slowly through the leaves, being careful not to add too much. Garnish with 1 chopped tomato and 6 chopped ripe olives. Serves 6.

Biscuit Tortoni: Heat ⅔ cup milk in a double boiler over hot, but not boiling, water until you see a film on the surface, then add ½ cup sugar and stir until dissolved. Now, in a separate bowl, beat 6 eggs slightly, and stir in a little of the hot milk slowly. Add remaining milk, transfer to saucepan and continue cooking, still over hot water, for 5 minutes, stirring frequently. Cool, mix in 1 cup finely crushed macaroons and ¼ cup chopped almonds which have been lightly browned. Whip 2 cups heavy cream until stiff, flavor with 1 teaspoon vanilla and 2 tablespoons sherry and mix gently into the egg-yolk mixture. Pour into refrigerator tray (or little paper cups), sprinkle ¼ cup chopped almonds over top and chill at a medium control on the refrigerator. Serve cold but not frozen solid). Serves 6.

Or, Fresh Fruit Bowl
Café Expresso

FRITTO MISTO

To eliminate the splatter of dipping vegetables into the batter and then into the hot fat of the fondue pot, you might fry them in the kitchen, then transfer them to a tray. The participating guests can then quickly dip them, and fry them to a golden brown, see below.

Green pepper rings
Mushroom slices
Eggplant slices
Carrot (stripped with a potato peeler for long, thin slices)
Celery stalks
Thick tomato slices
Parsley
Artichoke hearts
Green beans
Fennel
Sweetbreads, optional
Calf's liver, optional
5 eggs
1 tablespoon salt
1 teaspoon pepper
1 cup milk
1 cup flour
Bowl of flour
Bread crumbs, finely ground and seasoned with salt
    and pepper
Peanut oil or corn oil, about 3 cups

PART I   (IN ADVANCE):

The artichoke hearts, green beans and fennel are best if they are parboiled for just a few minutes, cooled and dried. Remove skin from the sweetbreads and cut into 1-inch cubes. Have butcher slice calf's liver 1-inch thick so that it also can be cut into 1-inch cubes.

With a whisk, or in blender, mix together the eggs, salt, pepper, milk and flour to make a batter. Prepare the bowl of flour, then the bowl of batter and last a flat plate of seasoned bread crumbs. Dip each vegetable and cube of meat first in the flour, then in batter, last in bread crumbs. All the vegetables and meat can be coated and placed on wax paper.

When ready to prefry, heat enough oil to 375°F. to fill a fryer at least 2 inches deep. Fry vegetables and meat until very light golden—not more than 1½ to 2 minutes. Drain on absorbent paper. Arrange them on platters; keep each variety in its own section. Fill the fondue pot ½ full of peanut or corn oil. Do not use olive oil because it has too penetrating a taste. Heat to about 375° on a deep fat thermometer. If you have no thermometer, test it with a small bread cube. Oil is hot enough for frying when it cooks the bread brown and crisp in 30-40 seconds.

PART II   (FONDUE POT OVER TABLE BURNER;
USE MEDIUM SETTING ON ELECTRIC FONDUE):

To protect the table top, place tray under table burner. Adjust burner so that oil will be heated to the boiling point throughout the appetizer course.

PART III   (EACH GUEST):

Using a fondue fork, dips the vegetables and meat in the boiling oil and fries them to a golden brown. Serves 6. Fritto misto can be served on the patio or in the game room before the main course.

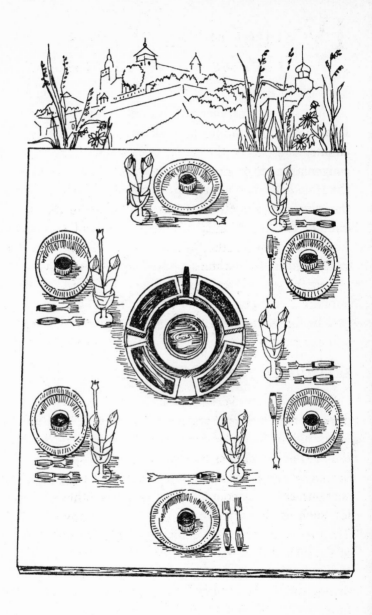

IV THE NETHERLANDS:
The East Indies in Amsterdam

Heading north to Holland means encounter with a people, country and cuisine that many of us have found the most congenial in all of Europe. And, granted the elegance of the Hague, the bright beauty of the tulips of Haarlem and the other enticements, astonishingly varied for its size, offered by the Netherlands, still the jewel of Holland remains Amsterdam, the bustling quaint city built on canals that total more miles of waterway than do those of Venice.

And in Amsterdam, one eats well. One of the special culinary excellences of this generally cuisine-generous city is to be found at the Bali Restaurant, 95 Leidstraat: there, you can partake of an authentic rijsttafel, or rice table.

11. A DUTCH RIJSTTAFEL FONDUE.

The Dutch discovered this intriguing repast during the days of their colonial empire in the Dutch East Indies (now Indonesia). It consists of a central dish of rice, surrounded by as many as twenty smaller dishes, which number includes a great many spicy meat and vegetable concoctions as well as counteracting tongue-soothing blanderies, such as slippery banana and unprovocative coconut. The procedure followed is this: you transfer the contents of the little dishes, one or two at a time, onto the big central heap of rice, consume them with both rice and condiments, and then cool your firey throat with deeply quaffed draughts of cold Dutch beer. Not all dishes need be spicy, and a hostess aspiring to her own rijsttafel can easily assemble a meal that's completely within the genre, yet not so overwhelmingly pungent.

A sample authentic rijsttafel menu consists of rice, soup, pork in soya sauce, meat in Madeira sauce, steamed meat, liver in its own special sauce, eggs likewise in sauce, sweet potatoes (relief at last!), bean sprouts, roast pork or chicken on sticks, fried bananas, vegetables in peanut sauce, cucumbers in sour sauce, and fried grated coconut; then, dessert, Dutch liqueurs, and Indonesian coffee. Impressive, what?

Not so impressive, however, as to warrant your shaking your head sadly and saying, Fine for Amsterdam, but no go for 105 South Main. I've discovered that a greatly reduced version of the rijsttafel adapts itself ideally to a fondue party menu.

The table setting is much the same as for a fondue Bourguignonne (you recall Salzburg and the Pension Nonntal!) with the fondue equipment in the center of the table, surrounded by bowls of rice, vegetables and condiments.

As to the condiments themselves: Indonesian sambals may be new to you. These are hot, hot seasoning spices with a base of fried peppers and vinegar. Some are more powerful than others: sambal oelek, for example, is almost liquid fire, while sambal roedjack and sambal asem are just plain hot. These can be obtained in most food specialty stores; if they're unavailable, you can substitute crushed hot Italian pepper. Very small seashells (oyster or mussel) make appropriately sized sauce dishes for these condiments. Guests can work out their own spice combinations, after they've assembled their plate of food, by adding small amounts and tasting—but it's wise to forewarn them as to what they're in for.

As indicated above, the drinking aspect of this Fun Fondue menu differs substantially from previous ones: First, *jenever*, or Dutch gin. Don't confuse this often very attractively bottled brew (I've Dutch friends who've used it for handsome gifts, in its ceramic container) with its British or American counterpart. Do *not* mix with a spot of dry vermouth, add lemon peel or an olive, and expect to come up with anything resembling a martini. In fact, don't mix at all. Drink Dutch gin straight, slightly chilled.

Then, with the main body of the meal, beer instead of wine; Heineken's is excellent and easily come by; finally, Curaçao is a fine post-rijsttafel post-prandial liqueur to be taken with the Indonesian coffee.

On the subject of rice

This is the second fondue menu to include rice (Fonduta in Chapter III, "Italy," being the first) and we'll be staying with it for a number of menus yet to come, so we had better tackle this vital subject right now, as the cooking of rice can be very tricky.

1. Since we're introducing the subject of the Dutch menu, I'll start with a Dutch rice and how it's cooked; it happens to be my own favorite method. Buy a box of Wessa (see Sources of Supply), a Dutch-milled rice imported from Holland. Each box contains 3 perforated plastic-like packages, with attached plastic handles. Submerge the package (each one serves 3-4) in a pan of boiling water; just enough so that it's covered. Tightly cover the pan, and let it simmer over a very low heat for 20 minutes. Then remove the package, and loop the handle over your sink faucet. The perforated package acts as a colander. Drain well, put the rice in a serving dish, fluff it up with a fork—and that's all there is to it: delicious and easy.

2. The Chinese method of cooking rice offers the added benefit of an unexpected by-product. Have you passed the time of night, long after guests have departed, standing over the kitchen sink scrubbing away on a rice pot, its remaining contents glued tenaciously to the bottom? I used to, but no longer. Let 'em stick. Go to bed. The Chinese deliberately let their rice rust and brown lightly in the bottom of the pot! They like the tasty little brown flecks in their rice dishes. And, being thrifty food-conservers, they'll add chicken soup to what can't be scraped out, reheat on the following day, and have soup. I've found this makes the basis of a tidy lunch: you can add all manner of bits and snatches of refrigerator leftovers.

Anyway, the Chinese method of rice-cooking goes as follows: Place 1 cup of long-grained rice in a strainer. Run cold water through it until the water runs clear, to remove excess starch. Cover the rice with about one inch of water in a *heavy* saucepan, and cook it, *un*covered, over a high heat. When the rice has absorbed all the water, its surface will appear to be pitted with holes. At this point, lower the heat to a simmer, cover the pan tightly, and cook for another 25 minutes. Then turn the heat off; the rice will retain the heat for at least one hour, and yields 4-6 servings.

3. Boiled rice. The rice: Uncle Ben's polished long-grained. Follow the package directions. It is as simple as that.

MENU

Saté Ajam (Chicken Kabobs)—recipe follows
Bols Jenever (Dutch Gin)
Kassblokjes Met Ananas En Gember (Cheese Squares With

Pineapple and Ginger): This is a typical Indonesian snack to serve with drinks. Simply place on a toothpick in this order: a chunk of pineapple, a cube of Gouda cheese and a slice of preserved ginger.

Sambal Oelek—Sambal Roedjack—Sambal Asem (Buy these condiments from your food specialty stores, or substitute crushed hot Italian pepper.)

Steamed Rice

Sweet Potatoes: Boil 6 medium-size sweet potatoes in their jackets until tender. Cool slightly and peel. Slice thickly and reheat in a skillet with 2 tablespoons butter. Serves 6.

Bean Sprouts

Fried Coconut: Use 2 3½-ounce cans of extra moist coconut; place in a skillet and fry until golden brown. Do not add extra fat. The coconut contains enough oil to brown. Serves 6.

Major Grey's Chutney

Curry Sauce (see Supplement)

Heineken's Beer

Haagse Bluf (The Hague Bluff, a typical Dutch Dessert): Beat 2 egg whites vigorously with electric mixer at fairly high speed, or by hand, until fluffy. Gradually beat in 1 cup confectioners' sugar and 6 tablespoons red, or black currant or raspberry syrup. Pile in sherbet glasses and serve with small butter cookies. Serves 6.

Bols Curaçao

Indonesian Coffee: Grind to a powder in an electric blender 3 cups of regular grind coffee. Do this 1 cup at a time. Add as much cold water as the coffee will absorb to make a very heavy syrup. Pour into a jar with a tight-fitting lid. Refrigerate for 24 hours. Strain through a fine muslin cloth to obtain about 2 cups of strong extract.

Scald 5 cups milk. Put 2 tablespoons extract in each demitasse cup and fill with hot milk. Serve sugar on the side. Serves 6.

SATÉ AJAM

    ¼ cup smooth peanut butter
    1½ teaspoons ground coriander
    1½ teaspoons salt
    1 teaspoon ground cumin
    4 medium-size onions, minced
    ½ teaspoon black pepper
    1 clove garlic
    1½ tablespoons lemon juice
    A pinch of cayenne pepper
    1 tablespoon brown sugar
    3 tablespoons soy sauce
    3 pounds chicken breasts, boned and sliced wafer thin into bite-size slices
    Peanut oil, approximately 3 cups

PART I (IN ADVANCE):

In blender container, place the peanut butter, coriander, salt, cumin, onions, black pepper, garlic, lemon juice, cayenne pepper, brown sugar and soy sauce; blend until smooth to make a marinade. Place the slices of chicken in a bowl and completely coat, on both sides, with the marinade. Cover and refrigerate for 3-4 hours. Remove from refrigerator and with a paper towel or spatula wipe off as much of the marinade as possible. Arrange the chicken slices, either flat or rolled, on platters and garnish with parsley.

Fill the fondue pot ½ full of oil. Heat to about 375°F. on a deep fat thermometer. If you have no thermometer,

test it with a small bread cube. Oil is hot enough for fonduing when it cooks the bread brown and crisp in 30-40
seconds.

PART II   (FONDUE POT OVER TABLE BURNER;
USE MEDIUM SETTING ON ELECTRIC FONDUE):

To protect the table top, place tray under table burner.
Adjust burner so that oil will be heated to the boiling
point throughout the meal.

PART III   (EACH GUEST):

First helps himself to the rice, which he puts on his
serving plate. He then spears a slice of chicken with the
fondue fork or skewer and dunks it into the hot fat, cooking
it until crisp, approximately 30 seconds. The fondue fork
or skewer will be very hot; therefore, the guest should
transfer his chicken to the bed of rice and use a second
fork to mix the vegetables, rice and condiments. Serves 6.

V MEXICO: Tequila and the Torrid Fiesta

What is Mexican cuisine? Mexican food, as we know it, is primarily the fare of the working-class Mexican—his are the tacos, the tamales and the tortillas. His aristocratic fellow-countryman favors a strongly French cuisine, and this predilection dates back to the brief but tellingly influential court of the Emperor Maximilian in the post-Napoleonic era. It explains the many fine French restaurants that flourish in the capital city, patronized by Mexicans both affluent and chic, who consume their fancy fare at a fashionably late continental hour.

No, the foods for our Mexican Fondue Fiesta can be traced to origins both mixed and ancient. Earliest of all was the highly-developed Indian civilizations that had long antedated the arrival of Hernando Cortez and his conquistadores in the early 16th century. Following the Spanish takeover, Indian foods and eating customs were absorbed into, but never obliterated by, the Iberian colonial influence that came to shape the face of Mexican culture. And, to complete the *mezcla*, Mexican-style cooking wended northward, in later days, into the kitchens of our own Southwest, where additional ingredients were added —so that fiesta recipes represent a combination of foods both ancient and relatively modern, from both north and south of the Rio Grande.

For many years, Eastern Airlines has flown to Spanish-speaking countries, and so, for many of us, Spanish has become almost a second language. I'm convinced that

81

speaking the language is almost an essential for tasting the true flavor of any country; this is especially true if you explore the local restaurants of the non-tourist variety, in out-of-the-way areas where the waiters speak no English, and where menus are either in the local language or non-existent. You may not be in a position to run to the nearest branch of Berlitz, so let my own Mexican experience be your guide.

We (the airborne sisterhood, that is!) have had many a rest layover in Mexico City, affording us time for leisurely strolling about and restaurant investigation; as a result, many of us have become devotees of the hot, spicy Mexican food. There's scarcely a day in the entire Mexican year when a fiesta is not in progress in some province or town. And of course all national holidays are celebrated on a country-wide scale with an incredible amount of merrymaking and eating; Mexicans are addicted to prolonged and colorful fiestas. The atmosphere is sheer holiday, and can be emulated, to some degree, by the American hostess who stages her own gay, informal Mexican fiesta fondue party.

12. THE FIESTA FONDUE.

Obviously, peasant Mexican table decor provides the ideal setting. The foods are served in much the same manner as the Dutch Rijsttafel, with the bowls of food circled around the fondue burner. Guests can mix and match their food to suit their personal tastes by the addition (or deletion) of chopped onion and hot, spicy sauce. A real *aficionado* will dribble some of the fondue on his chili beans and fried rice. But here again, a word of caution: I tried a Mexican fondue on some French guests who'd never been to Mexico, hoping to provide them with an amusing and tasty novelty. The French are not, as you know, water-drinking by habit, but my guests later told me they had spent the night calling their hotel room service for large pitchers of icewater. You've got to size up your fiesta clientele carefully.

As with the Rijsttafel, beer is the recommended choice for fiesta quaffing. Mexican beers are famous: Bohemia, Carta Blance, Superior, XX and Corona are all excellent, but expensive when imported to the U. S. So don't hesitate to settle for a good American beer.

Are you familiar with tequila? A tourist traveling in the provinces on a fiesta day will see the Mexican peasants standing at open-air bars drinking this fiery potation, which is distilled from the juice of a particular kind of maguey plant grown only in the Mexican state of Jalisco. Mexicans (and many visitors as well) take their tequila straight, a procedure accompanied by a fixed and felicitous ritual as follows: on the back of one hand, a sprinkle of salt, and a slice of lime between thumb and forefinger. In the other hand, a shot glass of tequila. First, lick the back-of-the-hand salt; second, gulp the tequila down fast; third, bite into the slice of lime. All done in rapid tempo. Heady and delicious. Try it once, if you like, at a fiesta fondue party and see how it goes. For the long pull, you may prefer a cold, refreshing Margarita, containing the same ingredients.

MENU

Margaritas: Moisten the rims of three 3-ounce cocktail glasses with the rind of a lime. Dip the rims into coarse salt. Put 2 jiggers Pepe Lopez Tequila, 2 tablespoons Bols Triple Sec, 2 tablespoons lemon juice, 2 tablespoons lime juice and 1½ cups crushed ice or ice cubes in blender container, cover and process at high speed (Frappe) a few seconds. Strain into the three 3-ounce cocktail glasses.

Salsa De Aguagate Para Sopear (Avocado Dip): Soften 1 8-ounce package cream cheese and add 2 tablespoons finely chopped onion. Halve 1 large avocado, remove seed and skin. Force fruit through a sieve, or blend in blender. Mix with 1 tablespoon fresh lime or lemon juice, ¾ teaspoon seasoned salt, and a dash of Tabasco (or to taste). Use as a dip for frito chips. Makes about 2 cups.

Mexican Fondue Monterey—recipe follows

Crusty Bread Cubes

Chili Beans: Sauté 2 medium onions, chopped, and 1

pound ground beef in 2 tablespoons fat until lightly browned, stirring often. Stir in ⅛ teaspoon pepper, 2 teaspoons salt, and 2 tablespoons chili powder. Add a 1-pound can of tomatoes and simmer very gently for 1½ hours. Add a 1-pound can of red kidney beans and simmer 5 minutes. Serves 6.

Arroz Mexicano (Mexican Rice): Sauté 1 chopped onion and 1 clove minced garlic in 3 tablespoons cooking oil until golden. Add 1 cup uncooked long-grained rice and cook until colored, then add 2 cups chicken bouillon, or more, 1 cup tomato purée, 1 tablespoon minced parsley and salt and pepper (to taste) and cook, uncovered, over low heat. After 12 minutes, check and add more bouillon if necessary. Cover again and cook until rice is tender and liquid is absorbed. Serves 6.

Condiments: Salsa (Sauce). Chop ½ onion in blender container, sauté in 2 tablespoons olive oil in small saucepan. Put 1 clove garlic, 3 canned green chilies, 1 teaspoon dried oregano, 1 teaspoon salt and 3 ripe quartered tomatoes peeled into blender container, cover and process until all ingredients are chopped. Simmer for 10 minutes. Serves 6. This sauce is easy to make and keeps indefinitely in the refrigerator.

Bowls of Chopped Onion.

Beer

Relish Tray: Celery—Carrot Sticks—Green and Ripe Olives

Spanish Flan: In a saucepan mix 1 cup white sugar and ½ cup water; cook over a low heat until it is light brown. Divide among 6 buttered custard cups. Beat 3 eggs lightly, mix in ¾ cup white sugar and ½ teaspoon salt. Add 3 cups scalded milk, stirring constantly, then add 1 teaspoon vanilla. Pour the custard mixture into the prepared cups and set them in a pan of hot water. Bake in a moderately slow oven (325°F.), allowing 35 minutes, or until a knife inserted in the center of the custard comes out clean. Cool the custard and carefully unmold it just before serving. Serve cold with caramel sauce.

Caramel Sauce: In a heavy skillet boil 1 cup water and 1½ cups white sugar until the syrup is golden. Remove pan from heat and stir in the ¼ cup water and 1 tablespoon butter. Bring to boil. Let cool and serve over the Spanish Flan. Serves 6. *Note:* One needn't read a history book to follow the trail of the Spanish Conquistadore: just follow the caramel flan recipes from Puerto Rico to New Orleans to Mexico.

Café Negro (Black Coffee)

MEXICAN FONDUE MONTEREY

    ½ cup onion, finely chopped
    ¼ cup green pepper, finely chopped
     1 clove garlic, finely minced
       Olive oil
       2 cups puréed tomatoes
    ¾ pound Jack cheese (Monterey), grated or minced,
          or use mild Cheddar
     1 teaspoon dry mustard
     1 teaspoon Worcestershire sauce
       Dash of Tabasco sauce, or to taste.

PART I   (IN ADVANCE):

Sauté onions, green pepper and garlic in a small amount of oil in the fondue pot. Cook until tender but not brown. Add the tomato purée and the cheese, stirring constantly with a wooden fork or spoon until cheese is melted. Bring fondue to a bubble briefly (a few seconds). Add mustard, Worcestershire sauce and Tabasco sauce, stirring until blended.

Note: Blender method. Chop ½ onion, ¼ green pepper and 1 clove garlic in blender container. Sauté in oil in fondue pot until tender. Put remaining ingredients (cut cheese into ¾-inch cubes) into blender container, cover and process until smooth. Add to sautéed mixture. Bring fondue to a bubble, stirring constantly.

PART II   (FONDUE POT OVER TABLE BURNER;
USE MEDIUM SETTING ON ELECTRIC FONDUE):

Adjust the burner so that the fondue will simmer slowly throughout the meal.

PART III   (EACH GUEST):

Spears a cube of bread through the soft side of crust and then dunks it into the pot, giving a good stir each time. Guests help themselves to the condiments. Serves 6.

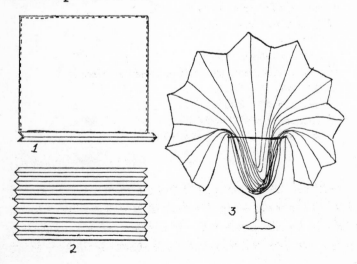

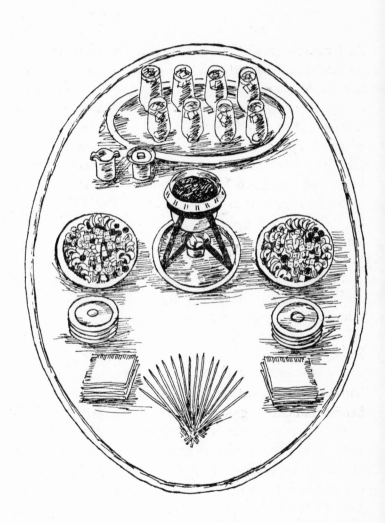

VI HOME HERITAGE:
Americana in Cheese and Chocolates

As I mentioned in the Introduction, I'm a Hoosier. My mother's family, the Heavins, were among the first settlers in central Indiana. And there, halfway between Indianapolis and Terre Haute, on the famous National Road now known as Highway 40, they built an inn, or as they were popularly called in those days, a tavern. It was called the Half-Way House, and it rapidly became famous for its hospitality and good food. For over 100 years, it was a mecca for connoisseurs of fine cooking. Many of the recipes for these celebrated dishes were passed down, from proverbial generation to generation, through the women in my family.

A number of these creations, I was later to learn, were quite sophisticated for rural Indiana. Behind the inn were a large herb garden laid out in a geometric pattern, an extensive and productive orchard, and a vegetable garden, all of which yielded an abundance of fresh provender. This wide variety of food and herbs, prepared with the natural Southern instinct for good food and the equally inherent tradition of gracious hospitality, contributed much to the renown of our family establishment. As early as 1840, Henry Ward Beecher made a special effort to stay at the Half-Way House on his trips through central Indiana. He was much struck, I'm told, by the beauty of the herb garden and orchard, both of which were laid out by Reuben Ragan, the first president of the Indiana Horticultural Society, Beecher's close friend, and one of my own forebears.

What were the specialties of the house? They sound very Southern indeed: fried chicken, sourdough bread, sugar-cured ham, egg noodles, and a special herb sauce for savory pies. And such was the reputation of this ancestral tavern of mine that the stagecoach traveling between Indianapolis and Terre Haute exerted itself in order to get its passengers over the thirty-five miles of mud and corduroy road to the Half-Way House in time for supper. There, in cold weather, stiff and sometimes nearly frozen passengers were ushered in before a crackling fire, and given large mugs of hot mulled wines to help them thaw out.

While yet a child, I'd heard stories galore of this early inn and the famous foods for which it was known far and wide. Martin Van Buren had been a guest there, and some members of the family claim—with every likelihood of its being so, given the location—that Lincoln stayed at the Half-Way House on his first trip to Washington.

So, when I came across Van Buren and Lincoln and Beecher in my childhood history studies, I paid shocking little attention to the Free Soil issue, or the slavery problem, or the gold standard, as I was supposed to. No; I was conjuring up pictures of these great men of an earlier era during their sojourns at the Half-Way House. Did my great-great-aunt Betsy serve her famous fried chicken to Van Buren? Did Lincoln get any of the sourdough bread? Had my great-grandmother actually *met* Lincoln as she waited on his table at the inn? Understandably, I think, my sense of American history was inextricably interwoven with my forefathers' inn, their notable guests, and their famous food. What more natural than that I continue my constant search for early American recipes?

American cookery has been maligned for so many years, both in this country and abroad, that I think it only fair that I try to set matters aright by creating one early American fun fondue party from the best of my native collection.

13. AN EARLY AMERICAN FUN FONDUE PARTY: WELSH RAREBIT.

Early American culinary research often dips far back into legends, as in the case of Welsh Rarebit. The experts who insist the dish is rarebit, and not rabbit, say that the word is derived from the fact that the dish is "a rare bit of gastronomical pleasure."

MENU

Mint Juleps: Fill a 10-ounce collins glass with finely crushed ice and set aside. Strip leaves from 2 sprigs of fresh mint, place leaves in mixing glass and sprinkle with 1 teaspoon super-fine granulated sugar. Macerate with muddler to release mint flavor. Add a splash of seltzer and 3 ounces bourbon whiskey. Stir gently, then strain into the prepared Collins glass, over the ice. Work a barspoon up and down in the mixture, until the outside of the glass begins to frost. Top with a splash of rum, 2 sprigs fresh mint, a cherry, and serve with straws. Do not touch the glass with warm hands; use a towel while handling, to facilitate frosting.

Hors d'Oeuvre Variés: One of my favorite hors d'oeuvre variés is an antique pressed glass platter outlined with old-fashioned deviled eggs, and the center filled with shrimps and Sauce Suzee.

Old-Fashioned Deviled Eggs: Cut 8 hard-cooked eggs in

halves lengthwise; remove yolks. Press egg yolks through a fine sieve or use a blender; blend in ¼ cup mayonnaise or salad dressing, 2 teaspoons heavy cream, 2 teaspoons vinegar, 2 teaspoons prepared mustard, ½ teaspoon sugar, ½ teaspoon salt, and ⅛ teaspoon black pepper. Spoon mixture into a cake-decorating bag with a star tip and stuff the egg whites with this mixture.

Cooked Shrimps with Sauce Suzee: See Ch. II, Sect. 6; sauces for *Fondue Bourguignonne.*

Fondue Bourguignonne.

American Welsh Rarebit Fondue—recipe follows

Toasted Cubes of Sourdough or Batter Breads See Index.

Beer

Hoosier Wilted Lettuce Salad: Fry 4 slices diced bacon until crisp. Remove crisp bacon pieces and drain on paper toweling. To the bacon fat add ½ cup cider vinegar, ½ cup water and 1 teaspoon sugar, and bring mixture to a boil. Place 1 medium head of iceberg lettuce, torn into bite-size pieces, (or 6 cups young, tender leaf lettuce) in a salad bowl. Top with ½ cup onion rings and 3 sliced hard-cooked eggs. Pour hot vinegar mixture over salad until well mixed. Sprinkle reserved bacon pieces over the top. Serve immediately. Makes 6 servings.

Tennessee Jam Cake: Cream together ½ pound butter and 2 cups granulated sugar; add 4 well-beaten eggs. Combine 1 cup buttermilk and 1 teaspoon soda. Combine 3 cups sifted flour with 1 teaspoon cocoa, 1 teaspoon cinnamon, 1 teaspoon nutmeg and ¼ teaspoon cloves. Alternately mix the milk and flour (reserve 2 tablespoons) in the sugar, butter and eggs. Add 1 cup seedless blackberry jam. Coat 1 cup nuts and 1 cup raisins

with reserved flour and add to batter. Bake in greased
10″ spring form (angel-food cake pan) for 1 hour at
350°F., or until cake tester comes out clean.

Butter Frosting for Tennessee Jam Cake: Cream ⅓ pound
confectioners' sugar with ¼ pound soft butter and ⅛
teaspoon salt. Blend in 1 teaspoon vanilla, 2 tablespoons
milk and ⅔ pound confectioners' sugar. Gradually stir
½ tablespoons milk into frosting until desired spreading
consistency is reached. Enough frosting for one 9″ or
10″ cake.

Alternate: A standard confectioners' sugar recipe can
be used for butter frosting, substituting orange juice and
the juice of ½ lemon for milk. The grated orange and
lemon rind can be added to the frosting.

Or, Bowl of Red Apples
Coffee

AMERICAN WELSH RAREBIT FONDUE

½ cup butter
2 teaspoons Worcestershire sauce
1 teaspoon salt
1 teaspoon paprika
½ teaspoon dry mustard
1 pound sharp Cheddar cheese, coarsely grated
1 cup ginger ale, or beer
2 eggs, slightly beaten

PART I   (IN ADVANCE):

Melt butter in fondue pot over low heat, add the Worcestershire sauce, salt, paprika, the dry mustard, and
cheese, stirring constantly with a wooden fork or spoon
until cheese is melted. Bring fondue to a bubble briefly

(a few seconds). Add ginger ale or beer, then eggs, stirring until blended. Continue to cook until thick.

Note: For blender preparation, see Chapter I, Fondue Cookery Clues: Cheese, Step 9. Melt butter with the liquid in the fondue pot.

PART II   (FONDUE POT OVER TABLE BURNER;
USE LOW SETTING ON ELECTRIC FONDUE):

Adjust the burner so that the fondue will simmer slowly throughout the meal.

PART III   (EACH GUEST):

Spears a cube of bread through soft side of crust and then dunks it into the pot, giving a good stir each time. Serves 6 as main dish or 10-12 as an appetizer.

14. CHOCOLATE FONDUES (SWEET AND BITTER)

Have you been wondering when, if ever, the subject of chocolate fondues would arise? And why not in Switzerland, where we assumed they came from, as they're usually known as *Swiss* chocolate fondues? The fact is that they originated right here, in the test kitchens of the Switzerland Association on Madison Avenue, where the dessert was created to promote Toblerone, a Swiss milk-chocolate candy bar containing honey, crushed almonds and other flavorings. So chocolate fondue may properly be called a stepchild of Swiss cuisine.

Ingenious American hostesses quickly adopted the fondue and changed the ingredients to create several versions of the original recipe.

A chocolate fondue works on the same principle as a

cheese fondue, except that instead of bread, delicious cubes of cake, lady fingers and fruits are dunked in the chocolate.

Chocolate fondue can be served as an ending to a light meal, but most people agree that a chocolate fondue buffet is a party meal for all ages. Whether it be an afternoon coffee jamboree, a dessert table for a progressive dinner party, or just for fun, guests will appreciate the novelty of a chocolate fun fondue party. It is a great entertainment idea to amuse teenagers. And it's so easy to prepare that my eight-year old niece, who dearly loves to cook, makes it for her playhouse friends. Even we stewardesses, brainwashed to curb a sweet tooth since our training school days, like to steal down the road of wicked, wonderful self-indulgence and eat chocolate fondue.

Dessert buffet entertaining has become very popular in this country. Buffet, literally translated from the French, means "sideboard" or "cupboard." In French culinary language, a buffet indicates a large tiered table on which various dishes have been arranged in a decorative manner.

A chocolate fun fondue party buffet has the decorative dazzle of a colorful work of art, and a party buffet for twelve is a simple planning matter. One warning note: since all dessert fondues contain sugar, they scorch easily. Use the lowest setting on your electric fondue pot for perfect results.

First, you'll need two fondue burners, chafing dishes, or candle-warmers—one at each end of the table. Ideally, one pot should be filled with milk chocolate fondue, and the other with a bitter chocolate fondue. Rather like passing a box of assorted chocolates with each guest having a choice. Arrange fondue forks and platters of dunkables near each pot. Line up dessert plates, napkins and silver in the order in which they will be needed.

What with all of the selecting and dunking in full swing, you may decide to set up the coffee at a separate table or sideboard, cutting down on quantities of confusion. Actually, what more harmonious counterpoint, of a hot summer's day, to chocolate fondue than a frosted glass of iced coffee? And summer is, in its way, an ideal season for a party focused on fondue de chocolat: fresh fruit's at its best, and everyone feels the cooler for the colorful table and chilled coffee. On the other hand, *vive* the wintertime fondue party as well, especially when, as should be the case, small glasses of kirsch and mugs of coffee, hot this time, are part of the scene.

MENU

Dark Chocolate Fondue—recipe follows
Milk Chocolate Fondue—recipe follows
Angel Food Cake Supreme or Raspberry Tea Cake Ring: see index for recipes; or substitute lady fingers or wedges of pound cake.
Fruit Platters: Strawberries, Fresh Peach Slices, Orange Sections, Canned Pineapple Chunks, Stemmed Maraschino Cherries, and Bananas and Pitted Dates.
Allow about 10 to 12 pieces of fruit and cake per person.
Iced Coffee

DARK CHOCOLATE FONDUE

9 ounces of Swiss milk chocolate with nougat, broken into pieces
1 ounce unsweetened baking chocolate
1½ cups light cream
2 ounces kirsch, cognac, or orange cointreau

PART I   (IN ADVANCE):

Melt chocolate in cream over medium heat, stirring frequently. When blended, add liquor and continue stirring until smooth.

PART II   (FONDUE POT OVER TABLE BURNER;
USE LOW SETTING ON ELECTRIC FONDUE):

Adjust the burner so that the fondue will be warm without simmering throughout the dessert course.

PART III   (EACH GUEST):

Spears dunkables and twirls in the fondue, using a circular motion, and then dunks. Serves 6.

MILK CHOCOLATE FONDUE

Five 3¾-ounce bars milk chocolate, broken into pieces
1 cup heavy cream
2 ounces brandy, optional

PART I   (IN ADVANCE):

Melt the chocolate in the cream in the fondue pot over medium heat, stirring frequently. When blended, add the optional brandy and continue stirring until smooth.

PART II   (FONDUE POT OVER TABLE BURNER;
USE LOW SETTING ON ELECTRIC FONDUE):

Adjust the burner so that the fondue will be warm without simmering.

PART III   (EACH GUEST):

Spears dunkables and twirls in the fondue, using a circular motion, and then dunks. Serves 6.

15. OLDSTYLE COOKBOOK BAKED CHEESE FONDUES: MRS. CURTIS'S CHEESE FONDUE

Back in the introduction to this book, I told you that my entertaining bachelor friend returned to New York in the fifties with news of his first Swiss Cheese Fondue, and urged me to find an American equivalent. At that time, my research yielded nothing comparable. But what I *did* find, stored away in my antique cookbook collection, were Mrs. Curtis' baked fondues.

Just about the most reliable source of elegant recipes in the early 1900's was *Household Discoveries and Mrs. Curtis' Cook Book*. A collector's item if ever there was one, because the book was never offered for sale in bookstores, and could be purchased only through "authorized solicitors" or directly from the publishers. Such exclusivity!

Mrs. Curtis, the guiding mentor, had surprising flair and imagination: she devoted a special section of her book to the favorite recipes of Mrs. William Howard Taft, the then first lady, and of wives of other political leaders of the day.

Mrs. Curtis' interpretation of fondue may not correspond

to the fun/flame/saucery variety that now holds the center of the international gourmet stage, but she was well within her rights, inasmuch as fondues in classic French cuisine were originally baked dishes of melted cheeses and bread-crumbs, related to the soufflé family.

MENU

Consommé: Cover 3 pounds lean beef with 3 quarts water, and simmer 4 hours. Add 1 carrot, 1 turnip, 1 parsnip, 1 onion, 1 red pepper, 1 tablespoon whole cloves, 1 table-spoon chopped parsley, and 4 stalks celery, and cook 1 hour longer. Strain and let stand over night. Next day skim off the grease, add the white and shell of one egg to clear it, boil up, strain again, and serve with imperial sticks.

Mrs. Curtis's Cheese Fondue No. I—recipe follows

Spinach Cooked Without Water: Young, tender spinach can be cooked without water. When well washed, put in a stewpan over the fire; cover, and cook for 10 minutes. Turn it several times during the cooking. Put it in a chopping bowl and mince fine. Return to the stewpan and add seasonings, allowing for ½ peck spinach, 2 generous tablespoons butter and a teaspoonful salt. Simmer 10 minutes; if very tender, 5 minutes will be sufficient.

Apple Sherbet: Put on to boil 2 cups sugar, 1 quart water, and chipped rind of 1 lemon. Pare, core, and quarter 1 pound apples, add them to the syrup, and cook until tender; press through a fine sieve, add the juice of 2 lemons, and, when cold, freeze the same as ice cream. Beat the white of 1 egg until frothy, add a tablespoon powdered sugar, and beat until white and stiff. Remove the dasher, stir in the meringue, and repack. *Note:* The egg white and powdered sugar are to be added when the sherbet has been frozen to a mush.

French Coffee: There are a number of pots on the market for making French coffee; any of them are suitable, provided they contain a fine strainer, which holds the coffee and prevents the grounds from getting into the infusion. To make coffee in this fashion, put 1 cup finely ground coffee into the strainer, which is generally set into the mouth of the pot; place the pot on the stove and slowly pour 6 cups boiling water over the grounds, allowing it to filter through. If you wish to have the coffee stronger, pour out the infusion and pour it a second time over the grounds. Serve hot. (You can keep it hot over a tiny flame, but don't let it boil.)

MRS. CURTIS'S CHEESE FONDUE, No. 1

1⅓ cups soft, stale bread crumbs
6 ounces of cheese (1½ cups grated cheeese or 1⅓ cups cheese grated fine or cut into small pieces)
4 eggs
1 cupful of hot water
½ teaspoonful salt

Mix the water, bread crumbs, salt and cheese; add the yolks thoroughly beaten; in this mixture cut and fold the whites of eggs beaten until stiff. Pour into a buttered baking dish and cook 30 minutes in a moderate oven. Serve at once.

The preceding recipe follows the original, but here's the updated version. Preheat oven to 350°. Beat egg whites stiff but not dry; set aside. Put bread (about 3 slices), water and salt into blender container, cover and turn on blender. Add egg yolks and blend until smooth. Stop blender, add cheese and turn on motor until cheese is coarsely grated. Fold mixture into beaten egg whites. Pour into buttered 2-quart baking dish and bake 30 minutes.

16. MRS. CURTIS AGAIN, BY POPULAR DEMAND

This baked fondue menu, like the preceding one, is a faithful replica of the turn-of-the-century ones in Mrs. Curtis's historic cookbook.

MENU

Tomato Soup: Place a saucepan with 2 tablespoonsful butter and 2 tablespoonsful finely-chopped onion over the fire; cook 5 minutes; add 1 bay leaf, 10 peppers*, 1 tablespoonful chopped ham, and 1 tablespoonful flour; stir and cook 2 minutes; add 1 can tomatoes (1 quart); stir and cook 5 minutes; add 1 teaspoonful salt, 3 cupfuls stock (brown), and dash McIlhenny's Tabasco Sauce; cook 10 minutes, then press the soup through a sieve and serve with toasted bread cut into dice.

* 10 peppers means 10 peppercorns.

Brown Stock for Tomato Soup: Cut in rather small pieces all the meat from 10 pounds of shin beef; break the bone in pieces, and put into a large pot with 3 slices bacon, 4 onions, 3 carrots, 1 turnip, 1 bunch celery, 1 sprig parsley, 1 sprig thyme, 2 tablespoons salt, 12 cloves, 1 teaspoon pepper, 2 tablespoons butter and 1 cup cold water. Set it over a brisk fire, stirring frequently to prevent burning. Cook until the juice from the meat and vegetables begins to thicken. Then add 7 quarts cold water, set it back on the fire, where it will simmer slowly for 6 hours, skimming very often. Strain carefully through a fine sieve, not bruising the vegetables. Next morning skim off the fat. You can make a variety of soups from this stock by adding to it macaroni, Italian paste, or finely-cut vegetables.

Mrs. Curtis's Cheese Fondue No. II—recipe follows

Summer Salad: Slice 6 tomatoes, 3 cucumbers and 2 green apples; chop 1 onion and 3 green peppers finely. Blend with a French dressing.

Strawberry Ambrosia: Select large, ripe strawberries. Arrange in a glass bowl with alternate layers coarsely chopped pineapple. Sprinkle between layers plenty of powdered sugar and freshly grated coconut, then pour over top 1 cup orange juice. Set on ice, and serve very cold. From Mrs. J. S. Sanders, wife of the Governor of Louisiana.

Tea: Water for tea should be used when it has just reached the boiling point. Teas are of differing strengths, but a safe rule is 1 teaspoon dry tea to ½ pint boiling water. Scald the pot, put in dry tea, and cover closely. Let stand 3 to 6 minutes and strain off into another hot pot. A wadded cosy keeps the tea hot for a long time.

MRS. CURTIS'S CHEESE FONDUE, No. 2

1½ cups hot milk
1⅓ cups soft, stale bread crumbs
1 tablespoonful butter
4 eggs
⅓ pound cheese (1⅓ cups grated cheese or 1 cup cheese cut into small pieces)
½ teaspoon salt

Mix the hot milk, bread crumbs, salt and cheese; add the yolks thoroughly beaten; in this mixture cut and fold the whites of eggs beaten until stiff. Pour into a buttered baking dish and cook 30 minutes in a moderate oven. Serve at once.

Note: For the blender version of this fondue, put bread, (3 slices, broken into pieces), milk, salt and butter into blender container, cover and process. Add egg yolks while processing and blend until smooth. Stop blender, add cheese and process until coarsely grated. Fold mixture into stiffly beaten egg whites. Pour into baking dish and bake 30 minutes, or until a silver knife inserted in center comes out clean. Serve at once.

VII THE HAWAIIAN ISLANDS:
Fondue à la Aloha

My yen for the islands, their special lore and for Polynesian cuisine began in 1967 under special circumstances. My
airline was operating special military flights from the
United States to Vietnam, with rest stops at Honolulu,
Guam, Okinawa, and the Philippines. These were chaotic
days and nights, and our entire attention was occupied by
our in-flight care of our soldiers; we weren't passing the
time of day or night indulging in our customary pet pas-
time of hunting down new and unusual restaurants. But I
did find time to read, and it was during this time and under
these circumstances that I plunged into the Michener
books of the Pacific, the *Mutiny on the Bounty* trilogy, and
Captain Cook's *Journals*. They were the source of my avid
interest in Pacific history and Polynesian cuisine. Some
day, thought I, I'll manage to return to this part of the
world at my leisure.

And so it transpired, far earlier than I'd dreamed possible. In October of 1968 I found myself standing, on the
brink of a vacation, at the San Francisco International Air-
port and hearing the blood-tingling flight call: "Pan American World Airways announces the departure of Flight
Number One, for around the world." *No. 1 for around the
world!* We were going only as far as Honolulu, but my
profession, thank God, hadn't made me sufficiently blasé
for me not to thrill at the words.

Honolulu, Waikiki Beach, Pearl Harbor, the Punchbowl
—we'd seen them all before, during the Viet Nam flight

phase. But to me, the Islands will always be Oahu, scene of my initiation into the gracious and leisurely life of Polynesia. We checked into the Ilikai Hotel, and started to expand. You're *bound* to expand at the Ilikai, with its glorious squandering of space—on the luxuriant grounds, and in the high-ceilinged rooms, each with a balcony overlooking the smooth strand of Waikiki Beach.

Cuisine-minded as ever, we'd planned our arrival to coincide with one of the Islands' most durable institutions: the Royal Hawaiian Hotel's Sunday night luau, held on the lawn near Waikiki Beach. Here, under stars and palms, with the steady beat of the surf and soft music as background, is the ideal place to acquaint yourself with the enchantments of Hawaii's ceremonial native feast.

The pageantry begins with the opening of the Imu (ground oven) and the presentation, accompanied by chants and conch shells, of a steaming Kalua pig to the assembled guests. Thus commences a full two hours of fun and entertainment fit for royalty—at the very least!

Shall I tick off just some of the authentic Islands foods served in the course of that bacchanalian feast? Kalua pig (the savory curtain-raiser); chicken luau; laulau (bundle of Hawaiian food); baked bananas and sweet potatoes; coconut pudding; fresh pineapple spears; coconut cake (shades of Rijsttafel!)—and all the Mai Tais (rum punch) you can hold.

The Mai Tai is Hawaii's most famous drink. From the big hotel bars on Waikiki to the smallest bistros on the neighbor islands, natives and visitors alike have sung the praises of this "friendliest drink in the Islands."

And friendly it is, being a heady concoction of three varieties of rum, assorted fruit juices, sticks of sugar cane and pineapple (the omnipresent Islands staple)—none of which ingredients can be dispensed with if the authentic Mai Tai character is to be preserved. It is not a drink to be taken lightly, and is both loved and respected by seasoned drinkers long familiar with the age-old Polynesian rum punch.

It's a proverbial Islands saying that there are two ways of becoming a Kamaaina (long-time resident). The first is to put in one's seven-year stint, learning to know the Islands and their inhabitants; the second, so goes the saying, is to spend one afternoon on Waikiki Beach drinking three Mai Tais. We chose a middle road: lacking either the leisure for seven years or the capacity for three Mai Tais, we settled for two weeks, one Mai Tai apiece, and came off quite well. In terms of fondue, Hawaiian-style, we came off superbly. Starting with that first chicken Luau at Waikiki, I've developed a complete menu for a Luau fun fondue party. Being malihinis (tourists), however, we will *not* start out with the Kalua pig. (The pig will get full treatment, on an optional basis, immediately following the luau fondue recipe.)

17. THE LUAU AND A PORK FONDUE.

The setting. Earlier on, I spoke of the informal charm of fondue parties in general. Here with the Hawaiian luau, the right tone is set immediately by having guests sit on the floor. It adds to the authenticity and virtually compels informality. If anybody thinks he's at a silent Buddhist sitting, the goings-on will soon set him right. I suggest that you urge female guests on to the most comfortable and suitable attire imaginable; the muumuu. They've become so popular on the Mainland that those who don't own 'em can make 'em—if they're so inclined, on their friendly domestic sewing machine in approximately one hour. Does it seem presumptuous to request guests to construct special costuming for *your* party? It may, but remind your female friends of two things: muumuus are eternally useful as beach and housedresses, and the Fondue Luau really warrants a bit of ceremony, informal-style. As for the messieurs, blarney them into their most blatantly gay Hawaiian printed ahola shirts. For your own contribution to the haberdashery, proceed to the nearest Woolworth's, where plastic or crepe paper leis can be purchased for the proverbial song, and placed around the guests' necks, together with the all-purpose "Aloha!" greeting as they arrive. One last bit of etiquette, local-color division: everybody takes his/her shoes off.

Atmosphere can be created by Hawaiian music on the record-player—or have you some ukelele-players on your guest-list? In the old days the Polynesians played the ukelele, first brought to the islands by the Portuguese. It's much more dulcet than either guitar or mandolin; it's easy to play, and no harm done if one isn't an expert.

Costuming accessories and background having been settled, we turn to the table-setting. Obviously the floor-sitters aren't going to eat off your 28-inch-high dining table. So: nail three wooden planks together, using crossboards, and cover them with green crepe paper or a dark green tablecloth. In the Islands, they cover the paper with ti leaves; you can use fresh spinach leaves and gain the same effect. With two-way sticky Scotch tape, or with staples, the spinach leaves can be firmly attached to the paper or cloth. Don't cover the area where you're planning to place the food. Down the center of the table, lengthwise, run a row of flowers, and on each end of the table create a round grouping of bananas, oranges and avocados. (Polynesians are avid fruit-eaters, as well they might be, surrounded as they are by all of the tropical varieties of bananas, papayas, pineapples, avocados, and grapefruit. Vegetables run a rather poor second. Coconuts rank high in popularity among the natives for their sweet milk, cream, water and oil. As to meats, the local menu is dominated by pork and chicken.) The middle of the table is, of course, reserved for the fondue burner. Between the end-heaps of fruit and the burner, place bowls of fresh pineapple chunks. Use grass mats for place settings, and put a flower at the upper lefthand corner of each. Traditionally, luau food is for fingers and not forks; for the more adventuresome—you can bet they're the ones who ask for chopsticks in Chinese restaurants—place fingerbowls on the table. Now the scene is set.

I'm inserting a brief prefatory note on Kona, which seems warranted because of the peculiar excellence of Kona coffee, served either iced, as recommended below, or hot (see Source of Supply).

It's unfortunate that the tourist trade is largely restricted to the Waikiki area; an Islands tour, Carib-style, is easily arranged, and island-hopping is becoming increasingly popular. A too-little-known gem is the little fishing village of Kona. Within clear view, the fishermen begin to return in late afternoon with their catch of blue Marlin; the fish-weighing is a public ceremony, attended by tourists and townspeople alike. You can see it all, sipping an iced Kona coffee, under the spreading branches of a monstrous monkey pod tree overlooking the harbour.

And/or get up at dawn one morning and drive from the Kona to Hilo, via the Kona coffee plantations along the scenic coastline. Stop for morning coffee at a little village restaurant en route, and you'll be served a cup of steaming hot nectar together with a spectacular view of the countryside.

Interestingly enough, the Kona coast is the only area in all of the United States where coffee is grown commercially. The supply is of necessity limited, because, as the natives maintain, the secret of its excellence lies in the peculiar combination of climate and location: the high mountains of Mauna Loa catch the midday clouds, and form a natural umbrella over the western slopes that lead down to the sea.

MENU

Polynesian Drinks: Mai Tai, Chi Chi, P. K. or Planter's Punch.

Mai Tai: Mix well in cocktail shaker or blender 1 ounce each of light rum, dark rum, and 151-proof rum; 2 ounces pineapple juice; 1 ounce lemon juice; ¼ teaspoon triple sec (orange base); ¼ teaspoon orgeat (French almond syrup)*; ¼ teaspoon grenadine; and 1 tablespoon confectioners' sugar (optional). Pour over large (15-ounce) old-fashioned glass filled with shaved or cracked ice. Garnish with fresh pineapple slice, cherry and mint leaf. Makes 1.

* *Orgeat:* Bought in food specialty stores and most pharmacies in pint bottles, or make as follows: Pulverize in an electric blender 1 cup blanched almonds and 10 bitter almonds. Combine with 1⅓ cups boiled water (hot but not boiling) and 1⅔ cups milk. Let stand 10 minutes, then strain through 8 thicknesses of cheesecloth. Mean-

while dissolve ⅓ cup granulated sugar in ⅔ cup water, boil over high heat, skim well, and mix with almond milk, then add 2 teaspoons orange-flower water. Refrigerate. Makes one quart. Note: Orgeat keeps indefinitely in the refrigerator; I always make an extra amount to share with friends.

Chi Chi. Mix well in cocktail shaker or blender 2 ounces each vodka, pineapple juice, and lemon juice; 1 ounce coconut cream*; and 1 tablespoon confectioners' sugar (optional). Pour over tall glass filled with shaved or cracked ice. Garnish with fresh pineapple slice and cherry. Makes 1.

* *Coconut Cream:* Bought in specialty stores, or make as follows: Insert a sharp, pointed instrument into each of the three round spots at the end of the nut. Pour out and reserve the milk. With a hammer, crack nut into several pieces. Pry meat off shell. (Easy if you heat nut in a very hot oven before cracking it.) Grate meat fine. Wrap about 3 tablespoons of the ground coconut meat in a double thickness of cheesecloth and twist and press the package until the cream is squeezed out of the pulp. Put cream in a jar and repeat untill all the cream is pressed out. One coconut produces about ¾ cup of pure cream. Modern cooks in Hawaii have taken to grating the raw coconut in a blender; a great time-saver.

P. K. Mix well in blender 2 ounces pineapple juice, 2 ounces lemon juice, 2 ounces vodka, ¼ teaspoon orange Cointreau, and 1 tablespoon confectioners' sugar (optional); pour over tall glass filled with shaved or cracked ice. Garnish with fresh pineapple slice and cherry. Makes 1.

Planter's Punch. Mix well 1 ounce each pineapple juice, orange juice, lemon juice, dark rum, and light rum and

1 tablespoon confectioners' sugar (optional) in cocktail shaker or blender and pour over tall glass filled with shaved or cracked ice. Float 1 ounce 151-proof rum on top. Garnish with fresh pineapple slice, cherry and mint leaf. Makes 1.

Pineapple Chunks

Bowls of Macadamia Nuts

Lomi Lomi Salmon: Shred ½ pound smoked salmon by pulling apart with forks on a cutting board. Scoop out pulp and seeds of 6 tomato halves. Dice and combine with shredded salmon, 1 large chopped green pepper, 3 chopped scallions and 1 medium chopped onion. Refill tomato halves, heaping the filling to make a mound. Serves 6.

Luau Fondue—recipe follows

Chicken Luau: Brown a 3-pound frying chicken, cut into 8 pieces, in 2 tablespoons shortening; sprinkle with salt and pepper to taste. Add ½ cup water; cover and simmer until chicken is tender. Meanwhile, wash 1½ pound fresh spinach and remove stems. Cut leaves into 1-inch pieces. Steam in a small amount of water until spinach is tender. Drain spinach and chicken and combine. Add 1 cup coconut cream (see index) and heat but do not boil. Serve on a platter. This very rich dish will serve 6.

Sweet Potato Poi: Boil 6 medium-sized sweet potatoes in their jackets until tender. Peel and mash, beating until smooth. Season to taste with salt and pepper. Gradually beat in enough coconut milk° to make the desired consistency—one-finger, two-finger, or three-finger poi. (The consistency of poi varies with the amount of liquid used and it is named according to the number of fingers needed to get it from the serving dish to the mouth without dribbling it on the chin.) Serve in individual bowls. Serves 6. * To make coconut milk, heat one 3½-ounce can flake coconut and 1 cup milk until it reaches the boiling point. Allow to cool at room temperature. Strain through 2 thicknesses of cheesecloth, squeezing out as much liquid as possible. Discard coconut.

Steamed Banana Molds: Beat 3 eggs until light, using a rotary beater. Add 1 cup sugar gradually, beating thoroughly. When foamy, beat in ¼ cup cold water. Blend in 1 cup sifted flour, ⅛ teaspoon sifted salt, and 1 teaspoon sifted double-acting baking powder; add 3 medium-size thinly sliced ripe bananas, cut into quarters. Pour into buttered individual molds, having them ⅔ full; cover with lids or foil. Place molds in steamer or deep covered kettle with rack. Have water, to half the depth of the mold, boiling rapidly. Keep water boiling constantly and add more boiling water as needed. Steam for 1 hour. Unmold and serve cool. Serves 6.

Iced Kona Coffee: Grind coffee beans and make coffee your favorite way (drip, boil or percolator), sweeten with sugar if desired. Chill. Before serving pour over glasses of cracked ice. Add 1 ounce of coffee liqueur (Kahlua) if desired. Top with a dab of whipped cream. Delicious! Can also double as a dessert with the addition of the coffee liqueur.

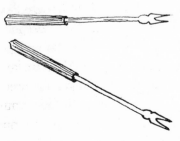

LUAU FONDUE

One 2- to 3-pound pork tenderloin
Soy sauce, preferably Kikkoman
Chicken bouillon, approximately 3 cups
½ teaspoon powdered ginger

PART I   (IN ADVANCE):

Brush pork tenderloin with soy sauce and let stand at room temperature for one hour. Then slice the tenderloin into paper-thin slices. Arrange the tenderloin slices, either flat or rolled, on platters and garnish with watercress.

Pour bouillon into the fondue pot, mix in the ginger and stir well. Bring to a boil.

PART II   (FONDUE POT OVER TABLE BURNER;
USE MEDIUM SETTING ON ELECTRIC FONDUE);

Adjust burner so that bouillon will boil throughout the meal.

PART III   (EACH GUEST):

Spears a slice of meat with the fondue fork or skewer and dunks it into the boiling bouillon, cooking it until well-done, 50 to 60 seconds. The fondue fork or skewer will be very hot; therefore, the guest transfers his meat to a spinach leaf and starts another morsel cooking. Serves 6.

Note: The traditional luau is a feast built around a whole pig baked in a fire pot. To prepare it, you must get up early in the morning, dig a hole in the ground, and line it with stones. Build a good fire in the hole, enough to make long-lasting coals, and add some stones, which are often family heirlooms, to get heated through. Dress a 100-pound pig (*don't* see Sources of Supply, please!) for baking and rub it well with rock salt. Place hot stones in its cavity, wrap in leaves and burlap, and lower the bundle in the pit. Wrap yams, bananas and breadfruit in leaves, and place them in the pit with the pig. Cover the pit with leaves and earth and steam all day in the oven.

If you think this sounds too much like work for people who favor the easy-going style of fondue cookery, you're right.

I have it on the best of authority that Hawaiians often rub the roast pig with soy sauce and powdered ginger before lowering it in the underground oven. But, assuming you don't want to cope with a 100-pound pig, the preceding fondue recipe is a reasonable substitute.

18. THE PUPU TRAY.

I assume you've exhausted the usual cocktail party formulae and variants on same. Well, despite earlier remarks in the full-to-bursting Swiss section of this book about fondues and cocktails being incompatible, I'm able, in good conscience, to recommend a wonderful cocktail-fondue party formula: the Pupu, a dexterous combination of Mainland and Oriental eating/drinking habits, and not to be pooh-pooh'd.

Mainland Americans are, by and large, thoroughly familiar with European hors d'oeuvres; they scarcely ever even mispronounce them any more, and an increasing number of cosmopolitanly-inclined countrymen spell it right on the first try. But now, blowing in from the West on easterly winds from the Islands, comes a new term for appetizer, fresh as to taste and visual appeal: the elegant and often elaborate pupu tray, offering no problems as to pronunciation, spelling or edibility.

The Hawaiian pupu party is in truth the Happy Compromise, combining, first, our oft-decried Mainland custom of heavy drinking along with a few munchables, and, second, the Oriental approach, which is to place the emphasis on eating, using drinks merely to complement the excellence of the food. The pupu-tray event is an eat/drink/be merry/simultaneously phenomenon.

Island hostesses draw on the varied, many-origined arts of the polyracial background of Hawaii in the preparation of the pupu tray; it's considered among the finest delicacies the Islands have to offer. You'll be able to emulate the entire menu with surprisingly few problems.

A word about the pineapple, as we've encountered it with the Luau, and as it appears both first and last on the Pupu Fondue Menu: the cool, sweet and refreshing pineapple is the golden fruit that symbolizes Islands hospitality. Cultivated in abundance, it's an apt symbol indeed. I'm including it both in the *Halakahiki Welcome* that serves as curtain-raiser, and in the *Pineapple Quick Tricks,* a bit of a fondue in itself, that terminates the proceedings. They are *not* interchangeable, as you'll see.

A final pre-menu comment: we'll use the fondue pot for this one rather than the tempura cooker, which is most often utilized in Islands cookery. Some of the pupu tray delectables—notably the beef, chicken or shrimp from which you'll select the chief ingredient—can be speared, traditional fondue-style, at the tables; other items, such as the Wun Tun, you'll prepare in advance on the stove and serve in style on a heated platter. And so to our Pupu Cocktail/Supper Party Menu and recipes.

MENU

Polynesian Drinks: Mai Tai, Chi Chi, P. K., Planter's Punch (see preceding menu)
A Halakahiki Welcome: This should be served just as the

guests arrive, signifying "Aloha—welcome; we're under-way." Bake 1 pound sliced bacon on a broiler pan at 400° until slightly browned, not crisp. Peel and cube 1 fresh pineapple into bite-size chunks. Cut cooked bacon slices in half. Wrap each pineapple chunk with a half slice of bacon. Secure with wooden pick. Place in shallow baking pan and pour (optional) Hawaiian dressing over. Marinate in refrigerator for ½ to 8 hours, if desired. Bake in oven preheated to 400°F. for 5 minutes or until bacon is crisp. Serve hot. Makes 25-30 appetizers. Serves 6-10. To serve, cut fresh pineapple in half lengthwise. Lay flat on serving tray. Stud rounded side of the pineapple with Halakahiki Welcomes.

Hawaiian Dressing (optional for Halakahiki Welcome): Combine ¼ cup pineapple juice, 2 tablespoons lemon juice, ½ cup vegetable oil, 1 teaspoon sugar, ½ teaspoon salt, and ½ teaspoon paprika; chill. Process in blender or shake vigorously before pouring over pineapple and bacon skewers. Makes ⅞ cup.

Macadamia Nuts

Coconut Chips: Buy in supermarket or make by following the recipe for coconut cream (see index). Instead of grating the coconut in the blender, grate it on the largest side of a cole slaw grater and spread out chips in shallow pan. Bake in moderate oven 350° for about 15 minutes until light brown, stirring frequently.

Lomi Lomi Stuffed Cherry Tomatoes

Pupu Fondue Hawaiian Sauce

Crisp Wun Tun: Combine ½ pound cooked fresh lean pork, 3 scallions, 1 teaspoon ginger juice (see Sources of Supply), 1 teaspoon soy sauce, and ½ teaspoon salt. Chop very fine; place 1 teaspoon of mixture on each wun tun square (recipe below) or buy ready-made egg-roll wrappers (see Sources of Supply). Bring opposite corners of the square together in a triangle. Then fold points at ends of the triangles, long sides toward each other so that they overlap slightly. Moisten corners and press together. As each wun tun is finished, place on plate and cover with a dry towel. If the wun tuns must wait longer than 30 minutes before cooking, cover with plastic wrap and refrigerate. Set a 10-inch skillet over high heat and pour in 3 cups vegetable oil. Heat oil to 375°. Deep-fry wun tuns, 8 or 10 at a time, for 2 minutes, or until they are crisp and golden. Transfer to paper towels to drain. Serve attractively arranged on a heated platter with Plum Sweet and Sour Sauce. Makes 2 dozen.

Plum Sweet and Sour Sauce: See index

Wun Tun Wrappers: Sift together 2 cups sifted all-purpose flour and ½ teaspoon salt. Make a small well in center and pour in 1 lightly beaten egg and ¼ cup cold water. With fingers, gradually mix and knead to a smooth, stiff dough. Divide dough in half. On a lightly floured surface, roll out the halves, one at a time, into 1/16-inch thick sheets, 14 x 14". For Crisp Wun Tuns, cut dough into 3½-inch squares with sharp knife or pastry wheel. If the wrappers must rest for any length of time, cover

them with a lightly dampened towel. Unused Wun Tun Wrappers may be frozen up to two months.

Pineapple Quick Tricks: Arrange rum, sugar and pineapple chunks around a pupu fire (a can of sterno set in a hollowed-out pineapple) and let guests use the fondue forks to dip pineapple chunks into rum, then sugar, and glaze them over the miniature volcano flame. Banana chunks can also be dipped and glazed in the same manner.

PUPU FONDUES

Pupu fondues can be made of beef, chicken or shrimp. Allow ¼ pound per person. Cut the meat of your choice in small bite-size chunks and soak for at least one hour in Teriyaki Sauce. Buy Kikkoman Hawaiian Teriyaka Marinade & Sauce or you can make your own according to the following recipe:

For each pound of meat or shrimp:
  ½ cup soy sauce
2-3 tablespoons sugar
  1 teaspoon grated fresh ginger, or ⅓ teaspoon ground
  1 tablespoon Bourbon or red wine
    Dash of monosodium glutamate
    Peanut oil, about 3 cups

PART I (IN ADVANCE):

Blend all ingredients in blender. Pour mixture over meat or shrimp and marinate at room temperature from 3-6 hours; drain before party.

Fill the fondue pot ½ full of peanut oil (approximately 3 cups). Heat to a temperature of 375°F.

PART II (FONDUE POT OVER TABLE BURNER;
USE HIGHEST SETTING ON ELECTRIC FONDUE):

To protect table top, place tray under table burner. Adjust burner so that oil will be heated to the boiling point throughout the meal. Place drained meats or shrimp in serving bowls around fondue burner.

PART III (EACH GUEST):

Spears cubes with fondue fork, or skewer, and dips into the hot oil; cooks to desired doneness. Removes cubes from fork or skewer to small appetizer plate.

19. FEAST LANAI FEATURES TERIYAKI

Hawaii, our 50th state, was settled by the Polynesians, although today little is left of their ancient culture. To those interested in the old, as well as the new Hawaii, I suggest renting a car and driving forty miles north of Waikiki to visit the new Polynesian Cultural Center at Laie where six authentic, lived-in native villages from Samoa, New Zealand, Fiji, Tahiti, Tonga and rural Hawaii provide a true glimpse of the principal Polynesian communities which remain much as early explorers found them centuries ago.

A Polynesian Feast (feast lanai, or patio feast) is served from 5:30 to 7:30 p.m. with a background of lively entertainment including grass skirts, ukuleles and the hula.

Continue on around the spectacular and peaceful shoreline road of the Island of Oahu past pineapple fields, foaming surf with intricately balanced surfboards riding the crest of the waves, past outrigger canoes anchored in secluded coves; then return to Honolu from the south and step back into the 20th century.

Hawaii today is anything but provincial. A veritable

Pacific melting pot, it embraces many ethnic groups who have retained much of their inherited culture but have exchanged cuisines to such an extent that the cooking style of the Islands has become an international blend, and delicious too! As a result, Islands supermarkets carry all the standard items found in Mainland stores plus a complete selection of Japanese, Chinese, Korean, Filipino, Hawaiian and Polynesian delicacies. It's this meld that's reflected in the Teriyaki Beef Fondue that follows: a subtle combination of the multiracial strains that characterize today's Hawaiian cookery.

MENU

Polynesian Drinks: Select from preceding menus.

Creamy Avocado-Macadamia Soup: Combine 2 cut-up medium-size ripe avocados (peeled and seeds removed), ½ cup macadamia nuts, 1 cup chicken broth, 1½ teaspoons lime juice, 1 small clove garlic and ¼ teaspoon salt in electric blender and puree until smooth. Turn into a bowl, and stir in 1½ cups heavy cream. Chill thoroughly. At serving time ladle soup into small bowls. Whip ½ cup heavy cream, and drop a spoonful on each serving. Chop ½ cup macadamia nuts, and sprinkle over each serving. Makes 6 first-course servings.

Teriyaki Beef Fondue—recipe follows

Chinese Steamed Rice. See index for recipe.

Island Green Salad: Wash, drain and refrigerate until needed 2 small heads leafy green lettuce and ½ bunch watercress, skins trimmed. Refrigerate 2 chopped scallions, ½ cup chopped celery and 3 cubed firm tomatoes. Rub a wooden salad bowl with a clove garlic and then discard garlic. Combine all ingredients in the salad bowl. Add the following dressing and toss lightly. Serves 6.

Island Salad Dressing: Combine ¼ cup vegetable salad oil, 1 tablespoon sesame seed oil, 3 tablespoons white vinegar, ½ teaspoon monosodium glutamate, 1 teaspoon sugar and 1 teaspoon salt in a jar and shake vigorously or blend in a blender. Add to Island Green Salad just before serving.

Bananas Foster: Cut each of 6 bananas into 4 pieces along the length of the fruit. Then heat the chafing dish, or flambé skillet, putting in 12 pats of butter and 4 tablespoons brown sugar. When this is filling the air with fragrance, add the bananas, and sprinkle with 6 dashes cinnamon. Stir the bananas gently to be sure that each is thoroughly cooked in the sugar and butter. When the fruit is tender, pour in ¾ cup rum and 6 teaspoons banana liqueur and flambé. The bananas are served immediately. A popular variant is to serve the flambéed bananas over vanilla ice cream. Have the ice cream dished up in individual portions while the bananas are being flambéed, so that both elements of this favorite dessert will be ready at the same propitious moment. Serves 6.

Hawaiian Coconut Cream Pie: Mix ¾ cup light cream, ¾ cup coconut cream (see index), 1½ cups water, ½ cup cornstarch and dash of salt together. Cook in a heavy saucepan over low flame, stirring constantly until thickened; simmer for 5 minutes to cook out the taste of raw cornstarch. Add 1 teaspoon vanilla and 1 cup freshly-grated, fresh-frozen, or canned coconut. Cool to room temperature. Pour into a 9″ baked pie shell. Cool, preferably overnight. Whip 1 cup heavy cream and spread in an even layer over top of pie. Serve thoroughly chilled.

TERIYAKI BEEF FONDUE

    3 pounds sirloin, or top round, sliced one-inch thick
    ½ cup soy sauce
    ½ cup water
    1 clove garlic, finely minced
    ¼ cup scallions, or onions, finely minced
    2 tablespoons granulated sugar
    2 tablespoons sesame seeds
    ½ teaspoon black pepper
       Peanut oil, approximately 3 cups

PART I   (IN ADVANCE):

Remove fat from beef and cut across the grain into one-inch cubes. Set aside. Combine the soy sauce, water, garlic, scallions or onions, sugar, sesame seeds and pepper. Blend in blender. Pour mixture over beef cubes and marinate at room temperature from 3-6 hours. Drain beef cubes well and arrange on platters. Garnish with watercress or parsley.

Fill the fondue pot ½ full of oil. Heat to about 375°F. on a deep fat thermometer. If you have no thermometer, test it with a small bread cube. It is hot enough for fonduing when it cooks the bread brown and crisp in 30-40 seconds.

PART II   (FONDUE POT OVER TABLE BURNER;
USE HIGHEST SETTING ON ELECTRIC FONDUE):

To protect the table top, place tray under table burner. Adjust burner so that oil will be heated to the boiling point throughout the meal.

PART III   (EACH GUEST);

Spears a cube of meat with the fondue fork or skewer and dunks it into the hot fat, cooking it to his taste—10-20 seconds for rare and 50-60 seconds for well-done. The fondue fork or skewer will be very hot; therefore, the guest should transfer his meat to a second fork. The first fork or skewer will have cooled sufficiently by this time, and the guest can start another piece of meat cooking. Usually three to four people can cook their meat at the same time. Serves 6.

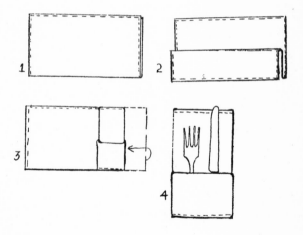

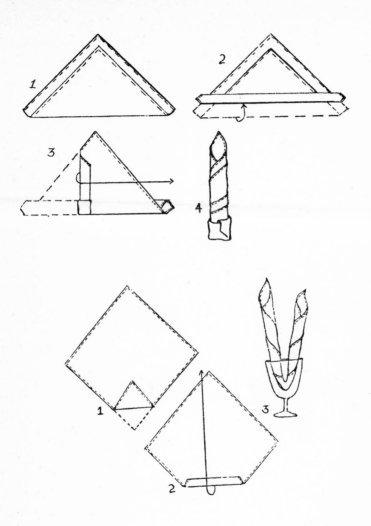

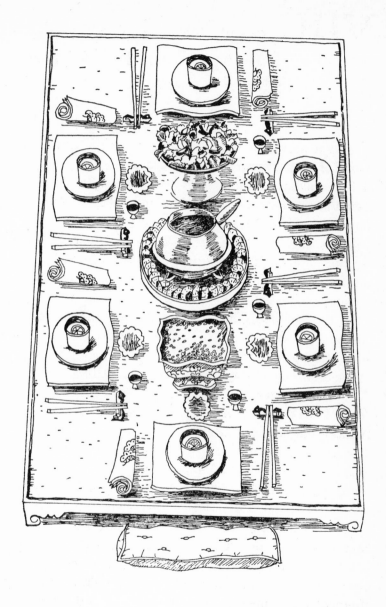

VIII GUAM AND JAPAN: The Tempura Touch and Floral Fondues

A word about Guam, the "gem of the Pacific"—incredible hybrid of natural paradise that it's always been, and base of ominous military operations that it has now become. Briefly, then, this southernmost of the Marianas Islands, 30 miles long and 4 to 10 miles wide, was discovered in 1521 by Magellan, belonged to Spain after 1696, was appropriated by the United States in the Spanish American War (1898)—and fell to the Japanese during World War II in 1941, being reoccupied by the U.S. in 1944.

On the paradisiac side, its wonderfully fertile valleys produce, in abundance, breadfruit, jakefruit, Ceylon-gooseberry, passion fruit, tamarind, and many other tropical fruits unknown in the United States, as well as coconuts. Yet Western culture, specifically military, is only too evident. (I don't want to present an ostrich-in-the-sand view of this exquisite spot.) B-52's come in almost daily from their raids on Vietnam—although one hopes that by the time you buy this book, this era will be behind us. One sees truckload after truckload of bombs hauled right down the main street of Agana, the island's rehabilitated capital, and polaris submarines return to their mother hen in Apra harbour, et al, et al. It's all extremely incongruous.

A midwinter New York-to-Guam jet flight with stopovers in San Francisco for a whiff of milder air, and mid-afternoon refreshment in Honolulu just before the 8-hour hop across the international dateline to Guam, is an experience that's got to be undergone to be believed; I simply can't describe it. It's like flying straight through the Looking Glass, and, in this our present fondue context, landing in a unique world where occidental and oriental schools of cooking encounter, mingle, and mutually embrace.

Side by side with the military goings-on proceeds the normal business of the day, combined with the wild social life of the island. Sampling: a dozen Sunday christenings, fiestas, marriage celebrations, funerals, cockfights. Often a funeral procession will merge with the cockfight-bound traffic. One dreads the all-too-soon day when exquisite and colorful Guam, sure to be an inevitable victim of the coming supersonic jet age, will become just another stopover of glossy hotels and mobbed beaches. Have you, perchance, the price of the jet fare and the time? Go now.

Early on in your stay, you're certain to encounter a fiesta. Guamanian fiestas come in assorted shapes and sizes; they seem to be held at the drop of a coconut—as is also the case, by the way, in Mexico, both reflecting Spanish influence. Each village has its own patronal saint's feastday, good for a weekend's mad goings-on, and there are twenty-three churches (i.e., patron saints) on the island! Then there are family feasts. The pre-wedding one's known as the fandango—carry-over, of course, from those two centuries of Spanish occupation. And hospitality on the most lavish scale is practiced to a degree that boggles the mind of the tourist, who, fortunately, isn't expected to reciprocate.

And so to food. It's the Japanese culinary influence that currently predominates, because after the war, this beautiful spot became the tropical playground of present-day

Japanese. In most restaurants, you'll find the Kikkoman's Shoyu Sauce (soy sauce to most of us) placed next to the Heinz ketchup bottle. Consequently I'm treating Guam as our first port-of-call on Japanese fondues.

One of the most enticing things about Japanese food is its sheer beauty. Care and ceremony, as we know from home decor and flower arrangements, constitute an integral part of Japanese culture; as much concern is expended on the arrangement of the food, its color components and even its shape as is given the cooking and seasoning. This, assuming you're willing to adopt the Japanese approach, makes it especially appealing as party fare.

Shrimp tempura is a specialty of many Guamanian restaurants where food is cooked at the table and served immediately. This *nabe* cookery (cooking at the table), which fits perfectly into our American scheme of fondue cooking, is actually an international style of entertaining in this era of scanty kitchen help.

20. TEMPURA SEMBEI FONDUE.

So why not stage a Tempura Fondue Party? I'm presuming a patio, or some other outdoor setting—but you can manage indoors as well. Picture a long, low table covered with lush greenery (fern, palm, or spinach leaves) illuminated by coconut shell torches in the background, with guests seated on floor cushions (you'll have needed these, of course, for our Hawaiian floor-seating fondue party), facing one another. As the diners rise and approach the table, they find plates handily arranged amidst fragrant plumerias, gardenias or hibiscus (any colorful garden flower may be substituted) tucked profusely into the greenery of the leafed tablecloth. The fondue burner is, as usual, set in the middle of the table, and individual tempura sauce-dishes are placed at the top of the serving-plates.

This entire table arrangement appeals to the internationally traveled hostess and to the archair gourmet as well. It conforms to the Oriental requirement that *all* the senses be appeased—that the eye be provided with a feast of color and beauty, that the appetite be satisfied—and that the mellow fragrance of flowers add its elusive aroma to that of the delicate foods.

Japanese meals are dissimilar to American ones in other respects as well. Not only do the participants sit on the floor, eat from low tables and use chopsticks, but the actual sequence of courses is different and produces unusual flavor combinations. Salads, for example, as we think of them, aren't served at all; rice or noodles take the place of bread. Green tea is the national drink of Japan, but often cold beer, or *sake* (rice wine), heated and served in tiny cups throughout the entire meal, are accepted accompanying beverages.

MENU

Chawan-Mushi (Steamed Custard): (Can be prepared ahead of time as a delightful prelude to a Tempura Fondue Party.) Beat 6 eggs slightly and add 3 cups cooled dashi (see below), 2 tablespoons sake (rice wine) or dry beer and 1/3 cup shoyu (soy sauce); mix well. Divide 3 large raw mushroom caps, sliced paper thin, among six 1-cup ramekins or ovenware bowls. Add 1 cup cooked peas, 3 thinly sliced scallions, 3 thinly sliced water chestnuts, 6 spinach leaves or 6 small watercress sprigs, cutting the greens into shreds and dividing as evenly as possible among the ramekins or bowls. Stir the egg mixture well and pour over the individual servings. Cover ramekins with lids or foil; set on rack in Dutch oven; pour hot water around cups 1" deep; cover to steam. Over medium heat, bring water slowly to simmering; reduce heat and cook about 10-15 minutes or till knife inserted off-center comes out clean. Cool and serve. Top each cup with a thin twist of lemon peel. Serves 6.

Dashi: This is the Japanese national soup stock. It can be bought in little envelopes, like large tea bags, and made by boiling in water according to directions on the package (see Source of Supply). Note: Chicken broth can be substituted for the dashi, but the taste of the custard is somewhat different.

Green Tea, Beer or Sake

Tempura Sembei Fondue (Cracker-Fried Shrimp)— recipe follows

Tempura Dipping Sauce—recipe follows

Sushi Rice: Wash 1 pound polished rice very well under running water 3 hours before cooking. Boil 2½ cups water, add rice, and bring to a rolling boil. Then lower heat and cook until rice is tender and water absorbed. Spread out in a shallow pan. Cool quickly by fanning. Mix in 1¼ cups white vinegar, preferably Japanese (see Source of Supply) and 3 tablespoons salt. Serves 6.

Japanese rice is sticky, not in separate grains, which makes it easier to pick up with chopsticks.

Oriental Salad: Sprinkle 3 teaspoons salt over 3 medium cucumbers sliced paper-thin. Chill thoroughly (1 hour or longer). Drain in sieve, pressing with paper towels to remove as much moisture as possible. Sprinkle 3 cups shredded carrots with ½ teaspoon salt. Combine

1 cup sugar and 1 cup white vinegar, stirring to dissolve sugar. Place cucumbers in one side of bowl and carrots in other side; pour vinegar mixture over all. Chill at least 1 hour. To serve, drain, reserving liquid to use as dressing; arrange carrots in center of cucumber ring. Serves 6. Note: This salad will keep for several days in the refrigerator. Cover and leave in dressing.

Japanese Fruit Dessert: A simple Oriental fruit dessert can be made with 4 cups of honeydew melon balls and 2 cups of sweetened fresh raspberries—appealing to the eye and refreshing to the palate. Serves 6.

TEMPURA SEMBEI FONDUE,
(Cracker-fried shrimp)

3 pounds fresh baby shrimp, 1½ inches in length
3 eggs
1½ teaspoons shoyu (soy sauce)
1½ cups sembei crumbs (see note)
   Peanut oil, about 3 cups

PART I   (IN ADVANCE):

Shell shrimp and remove the black vein, but leave the tails on. Open the shrimp with a sharp knife and flatten with a mallet. Beat eggs slightly; add shoyu. Roll sembei or whirl in the blender to make crumbs. Dip shrimps into egg mixture, then into crumbs, and allow to dry on a rack for 30 minutes. Arrange attractively on a platter and garnish with watercress sprigs. Pour oil into the fondue pot. Heat to a temperature of 375°F. on a deep fat thermometer.

PART II   (FONDUE POT OVER TABLE BURNER;
USE HIGHEST SETTING ON ELECTRIC FONDUE):

Adjust heating element to maintain proper temperature. Check temperature after several shrimp have been cooked. Use a bamboo mat or tray to protect table top.

PART III   (EACH GUEST):

Spears shrimp with fondue fork, or skewer, and dips it into the hot oil, allowing the shrimp to cook until nicely browned, removes the shrimp from fork and starts another cooking. Serve with tempura dipping sauce. Serves 6.

Note: Sembei are Japanese crackers of which there are many varieties, but the one to use is the small salty kind with a shiny varnished look (see Source of Supply).

TEMPURA DIPPING SAUCE

½ cup shoyu (soy sauce)
⅔ cup water
2 tablespoons sake (or dry sherry)
1 teaspoon monosodium glutamate
1 teaspoon ground ginger
Grated white radish or chopped chives

Heat together shoyu, water, sake, monosodium glutamate and ground ginger. Serve warm in individual sauce dishes. Sprinkle each portion with grated white radish or chopped chives. Serves 6.

21. CHRYSANTHEMUM TEMPURA

Most Americans' concept of a tempura, derived from Stateside Japanese restaurants, is shrimps dipped into batter and fried in deep fat. This is indeed one form of the genre, but in Japan, all kinds of seafood are used, as are vegetables and even flowers. Specifically, the flowering chrysanthemum and the squash blossom, incredible though this may seem.

For centuries, in northern Japan, a species of chrysanthemum has been developed for culinary purposes. But many florists' chrystanthemums serve just as well for cooking. (This'll teach you to eye these decorative blooms with a new glint!) Be your choice the cooking or the florist variety, you'll have no difficulty appreciating the pungent fragrance and flavor. Chrysanthemums, by the way, are also highly esteemed as among the most refined dishes of the tea-serving ceremony, and are used by the most discriminating tea masters.

Flower cookery is not restricted to Japan, incidentally. The Filipinos gather flowers from the sesbania and horseradish trees to use in their cooking, which reflects the combined influence of the Chinese, Malaysian and Spanish who successively settled in their country. And when Hernando Cortez arrived in Mexico, he found Montezuma and his subjects making extensive use in their cuisine of squash blossoms and other flowers. Even closer to home and not long ago, my mother, an amateur horticulturist, plucked some squash blossoms from the vines in her kitchen garden and deep-fried them for us. We considered them a Grade A taste-treat, second only to the first mushrooms of spring, the lovely morsels that are rated as one of the epicurean delights of French and Asian cookery, and which grow—small world!—in profusion around the limestone areas of central Indiana.

MENU

Chrysanthemum Tempura Fondue—recipe follows
Cucumber Sandwiches: Soak 12 thin slices cucumber for
   1 hour in white vinegar, salt and pepper to taste. Drain
   cucumbers thoroughly. Place cucumbers between 24
   thin rounds of buttered (fresh) white bread. Serves 6.
Watercress Sandwiches: Sprinkle 1¼ cups chopped watercress with salt and paprika and mix with ¼ cup mayonnaise. Spread between 24 thin rounds brown bread.
   Serves 6.
Japanese Green Tea

CHRYSANTHEMUM TEMPURA FONDUE

   6 medium-size chrysanthemums
   1 cup flour
   2 cups water
   Peanut oil, about 3 cups

PART I   (IN ADVANCE):

Cut the flowers, wash and dry on paper towels, and
place in upright containers. Prepare a mixture of flour and
water and stir vigorously until all lumps have disappeared.
Pour oil into the fondue pot. Heat to 375°F. on deep fat
thermometer.

PART II   (FONDUE POT OVER TABLE BURNER;
USE HIGHEST SETTING ON ELECTRIC FONDUE):

Adjust burner so that oil will remain at proper temperature throughout the meal. Pour flour and water mixture
over the chrysanthemums until a thin coating completely
covers all the petals. Bring the flowers to the table in their
containers.

PART III   (EACH GUEST):

Takes the flower by the stem and quickly dips them into the fondue pot. When the petals open out and become stiff, remove the flower from the oil. It is now ready to be eaten. Do not eat the stem or leaves. Serves 6.

22. IKEBANA: FRIED SQUASH BLOSSOM

Using a decor similar to that suggested in our Guam-based Tempura party, the hostess with a flair for the unusual might serve fried squash blossoms at a meeting of Ikebana International or of the local ladies' garden club, adding a new floral dimension to the organization's scope— or just for the fun and flame of it.

MENU

Fried Squash Blossom Fondue—recipe follows
Platter of Tea Sandwiches: See preceding menu
Japanese Green Tea

FRIED SQUASH BLOSSOM FONDUE

12 squash blossoms
1 cup flour
2 tablespoons cornstarch
1½ teaspoons baking powder
1 teaspoon monosodium glutamate
1 teaspoon salt
⅔ cup water
Few drops yellow food coloring
Peanut oil, about 3 cups

PART I   (IN ADVANCE):

Wash squash blossoms and remove stems. Let them drain dry on paper toweling. Mix the flour, cornstarch, baking powder, monosodium glutamate, salt, water and food coloring with a wire whisk until all lumps have disappeared. Dip each blossom into the batter and coat thoroughly and place on wax paper. Prefry the blossoms in a skillet in the kitchen by cooking in hot oil at 375°F. on a deep fat thermometer (or test using a 1½-inch bread cube which should turn golden). This batter has the advantage of staying crisp when reheated. Drain blossoms on absorbent paper and arrange attractively on a platter. Pour oil into the fondue pot.

PART II   (FONDUE POT OVER TABLE BURNER;
USE HIGHEST SETTING ON ELECTRIC FONDUE):

Adjust burner so that the oil will remain at the proper temperature throughout the meal. Arrange platter of blossoms near burner, which should be set on a bamboo tray or mat.

PART III   (EACH GUEST):

Spears the flower with a fondue fork and dips it in the hot oil to fry until golden brown. Serves 6.

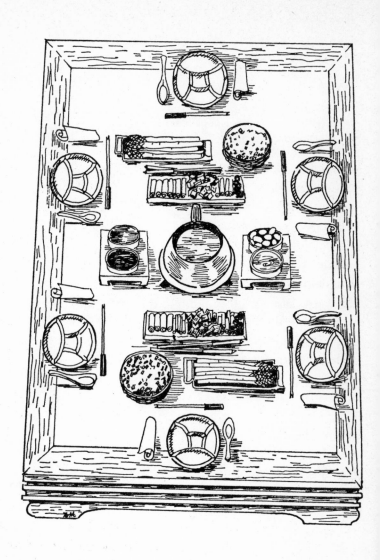

IX CHINA: The Mysterious Orient and Lightweight Saucery

23. *THE LEGENDARY FONDUE IN A FIREPOT*

Re-enter, at this point in our global fondue research, the ubiquitous Swiss. Many years ago (Legend #903, but authentic) a Swiss traveling in China was served a meal called "Chrysanthemum Fire Pot." The basic principle of diner-doing-the-dunking was so similar to Swiss fondue practice that, upon returning to his native Alps, he told a Swiss chef about it. The chef modified it, called it "Fondue Chinoise," and put it on his restaurant's menu. There it was discovered a dozen years ago by Konrad Egli, of New York's famed Chalet Suisse on East 48th Street. Herr Egli perfected his own version, renamed it, and introduced it to Americans as "Fondue Oriental."

Central motif: a chrysanthemum fire pot. In the middle of the table (a phrase you'll be accustomed to by now) stands the fire pot, an odd-looking vessel pierced in the middle by a thick metal cylinder whose base is filled with burning charcoal. Bubbling chicken broth half fills the basin around the "chimney" and the heated cylinder. The fire pot is surrounded by uncooked foods. These include sliced white chicken meat, pork, beef, shrimp, sole, oysters, calf's liver, celery, cabbage, bean curd and so forth. First, the broth itself is enriched by the meat being dipped in it at some length. Then the diner, holding each piece in chopsticks, dips the rest of the food into the broth, keeps it there a moment or two, and then dresses it in sauce. Sauces, rice and green salad are the perfect side dishes.

Fondue Oriental boasts many charms, and not the least of them is that it's far less fattening than most of the fondues we've examined. Another is that when the main course is finished, there's a residual bonus: the bouillon in which the meats have been cooked is delicious. Add a dash of sherry, and serve in small bowls. Sherry can be placed on the table in a large brandy-snifter, and each guest can lace his bouillon to suit himself. The snifter adds great style to the table, and adds a gourmet touch. (I claim no originality: I copied the idea from Perdita's Restaurant in Charleston, South Carolina, where they follow the same procedure when they serve their renowned she-crab soup.)

MENU

Fondue Oriental—recipe follows
Sauces for Fondue Oriental—recipe follows
Rice: See index.
Asparagus Oriental: Heat large skillet; add 2 tablespoons peanut oil and ½ teaspoon salt. When hot add 3 cups asparagus cut on the bias in thin 1½-inch pieces. Sprinkle with ½ teaspoon monosodium glutamate. Quickly heat the asparagus through, stirring constantly. Add ¼ teaspoon sugar and ¼ cup chicken broth. Cover and cook over high heat till just tender, about 5 minutes. Shake the skillet often. Serves 6.
Bouillon—Dry Sherry: Place sherry on the table in a large brandy snifter so each guest can lace bouillon to his own taste.
Fruit Pagodas: Unmold 2 one-pint cartons solid frozen vanilla ice cream by cutting away the outside paper carton with a knife. Place ice cream molds on a tray.

Decorate molds with a choice of pineapple cubes, preserved ginger, loquats, lichees, and kumquats by placing
the fruits on toothpicks and sticking them into the ice
cream molds. Preferably have the toothpick-speared
fruits ready to stick into the ice cream before you take
the molds from the freezer. Refreeze the molds. Serve
the molds at the table. They are beautiful and so easy
to do. Serves 6. Note: Soak raisins in rum overnight and
make a special rum-raisin ice cream dessert, using the
above toothpick method.

Green Tea

FONDUE ORIENTAL

Select a variety from the following meats, allowing a total of
½ pound per person:
   Beef, rump, fillet or sirloin
   Lean veal
   Pork fillet, or tenderloin
   Lamb
   Veal kidneys
   Lamb kidneys
   Calf's liver
   Sweetbreads
   Chicken
3 cups chicken bouillon

PART I (IN ADVANCE):

Soak kidneys and sweetbreads in cold water for ½ hour
before using; change water three times. Then drain and
dry. Remove all fat and hard cores from the kidneys. Slice
all the meats thin; the job will be much easier if you freeze
them first for an hour or so. Arrange the morsels attractively, either flat or, when possible, rolled on platters and
garnish with parsley.

Pour chicken bouillon into the fondue pot and bring to a boil.

PART II   (FONDUE POT OVER TABLE BURNER;
USE MEDIUM SETTING ON ELECTRIC FONDUE):

Adjust burner so the bouillon will boil gently throughout the meal. The bouillon must be kept boiling throughout the meal.

PART III   (EACH GUEST):

Spears one or more meats with either a fondue fork or skewer. Then transfers meat to service plate and dunks in a variety of the following sauces. Serves 6. *Note:* Pork should be well cooked while kidneys become tough if cooked too long.

SAUCES FOR FONDUE ORIENTAL

RED MUSTARD SAUCE:

    ¾ cup catsup
    ¼ cup water
 1½ tablespoons dry mustard
    1 teaspoon salt

Combine all ingredients; blend in blender. Chill. Makes 1 cup.

SWEET-SOUR SAUCE:

    ½ cup pineapple tidbits
    ¼ cup brown sugar
    ¾ tablespoon cornstarch
    3 tablespoons water
    ¼ cup white vinegar
    ¼ cup green-pepper strips

Drain pineapple, reserving syrup. Combine brown sugar, cornstarch, and salt. Slowly stir in water, vinegar, and reserved pineapple syrup. Bring to boiling; simmer about 5-7 minutes or until thick, stirring constantly. Add pineapple and green pepper, simmer a few minutes longer. Makes 1¼ cups.

TARTAR SAUCE:

> 1 jar (6 ounces) Tartar sauce
> 3 teaspoons sweet pickle relish, drained
> 2 teaspoons mayonnaise
> 2 teaspoons capers

Mix together and serve at room temperature. Makes 1 cup.

LEMON-CHILI SAUCE:

> ⅔ cup chili sauce
> grated rind of one lemon
> 1 tablespoon lemon juice

Blend together in blender and serve at room temperature. Makes approximately ¾ cup.

Arrange the sauces around the fondue pot in a circular fashion.

24. FONDUE CHINOISE, BEEF AND SEAFOOD.

These are alternate versions of Fondue Oriental (No. 23) described above. On a Chinese menu, rice wine is often listed as an accompanying drink. It's somewhat strange to the Western palate, and a pale dry sherry served as an apéritif is (to the uninitiated at least) a more agreeable introduction.

MENU

Apéritif: Pale Dry Sherry

Beef or Seafood Fondue Chinoise—recipe follows

Sauces for Fondue Chinoise—recipe follows

Steamed Rice: See index

Salad: Liang-Pan-Hsi-Yang-Ts'ai. Trim and discard the
tough ends of 3 bunches watercress stems. Wash the
watercress under cold running water, drop it into a pot
of boiling water, then drain and pat the leaves dry with
paper towels. With a large knife, chop the watercress
fine. Drain 12 canned water chestnuts and cut them into
⅛-inch slices. Then chop fine. Combine in a large bowl
1½ teaspoons soy sauce, 3 teaspoons sesame seed oil,
1 teaspoon salt, and 1½ teaspoons sugar and mix thoroughly. Add the watercress and water chestnuts and toss
them with a large spoon so that they are well coated
with the mixture. Chill and serve. Serves 6.

Mandarin Orange Dessert I: Combine 1 package instant
vanilla pudding and 3 cups milk following package label
directions. Pour in serving bowls; let stand till set, about
10 minutes. Serve with a topping of orange slices or 2
11-ounce cans (2½ cups) mandarin orange sections,
drained. Serves 6.

Mandarin Orange Dessert II: Mix 3 tablespoons cornstarch, 3 tablespoons sugar and ¼ teaspoon salt with ½
cup milk. Scald 1½ cups milk in top of double burner.
Add cornstarch gradually to scalded milk, stirring constantly. Cook, stirring constantly, until thickened and
smooth. Cover and cook 25 minutes, stirring constantly.
Cool and add 1 teaspoon vanilla. Turn into individual
molds that have been dipped in ice water, and chill.
Unmold and serve with orange slices or 2 11-ounce cans
(2½ cups) mandarin orange sections, drained. Serves 6.

Green Tea

SEAFOOD FONDUE CHINOISE FOR WEIGHT WATCHERS

- 1 quart bottled clam juice
- 2 cups dry white wine
- 2 cups water
- 1 large onion, finely chopped
- 1 large carrot, finely chopped
- 1 stalk celery, finely chopped
- 4 peppercorns
- 1 bay leaf
- 1 teaspoon salt
- 1 pound fresh shrimp (approximately 2 inches in length), peeled and deveined
- 1 pound fresh deep sea scallops, each cut in 3 slices
- 1 pound fresh lobster tails, cut in bite-size pieces

PART I   (IN ADVANCE):

Make a court bouillon by combining the clam juice, white wine, water, onion, carrot, celery, peppercorns, bay leaf and salt together in a large cooking pot. Cook over moderate heat for 30 minutes. Strain through a fine sieve. Reserve the liquid; discard the vegetables and seasonings. At serving time heat the court bouillon to a rolling boil.

PART II   (FONDUE POT OVER TABLE BURNER;
USE MEDIUM SETTING ON ELECTRIC FONDUE):

Arrange seafood on 2 large shells or border a platter with sea shells. Place bamboo mat or tray under table burner. Adjust burner so that court bouillon will boil gently throughout the meal.

PART III   (EACH GUEST):

Spears a bite-size piece of seafood, dunks it into the boiling court bouillon, cooking it from 1 to 1½ minutes, depending upon the size of the pieces. When the fish has been consumed, the court bouillon can be ladled into small rice bowls to satiate the weight-watching guest. Serves 6.

BEEF FONDUE CHINOISE

> 3 pounds beef fillet or sirloin
> Beef bouillon (about 3 cups)

PART I   (IN ADVANCE):

Have your butcher slice the steak paper thin, or do it yourself. Arrange the slices attractively, either flat or rolled, on a platter and garnish with parsley.

Pour beef bouillon into the fondue pot and bring to a boil.

PART II   (FONDUE POT OVER TABLE BURNER;
USE MEDIUM SETTING ON ELECTRIC FONDUE):

Adjust burner so the bouillon boils gently throughout the meal. The bouillon must be kept boiling throughout the meal.

PART III   (EACH GUEST):

Spears the meat with a fondue fork or skewer and cooks to desired taste. Then transfers meat to service plate and dunks at will in a variety of the following sauces. Serves 6.

SAUCES FOR FONDUE CHINOISE

SOY SAUCE:

> ¼ cup soy sauce
> 1 tablespoon lemon juice
> ½ cup water
> ½ teaspoon monosodium glutamate

Blend well and serve. Makes ¾ cup.

PLUM SWEET AND SOUR:

  ⅔ cup plum jam
  1 cup boiling water
  2 teaspoons dry mustard
  2 teaspoons cold water

Add the plum jam to the boiling water. Continue boiling until the mixture is smooth, and let cool. In a separate dish mix well the mustard and cold water to make an English mustard mixture. Just before serving, drop the English mustard mixture into the cooled plum jam mixture. Do not stir. Makes approximately 1¼ cups.

JET-GOURMET GREEN SAUCE:

  2 teaspoons dried tarragon leaves
  2 tablespoons tarragon vinegar
  2 cups mayonnaise
  6 peeled scallions, chopped
  ¼ teaspoon dry mustard
  Dash of Tabasco

Mix tarragon leaves and vinegar and let stand 30 minutes. Combine ingredients in an electric blender, cover and blend at high speed for 30 seconds. Chill and serve cold. Makes approximately 2½ cups.

TOMATO SAUCE:

  ⅓ cup minced onion
  3 tablespoons butter
  1 cup catsup
  ⅓ cup white vinegar
  ½ cup water
  2 tablespoons brown sugar
  2 teaspoons prepared mustard
  2 tablespoons Worcestershire sauce

Sauté onion in butter till tender. Add remaining ingredients and simmer, covered for 10 minutes, let cool and serve. Makes approximately 2¼ cups.

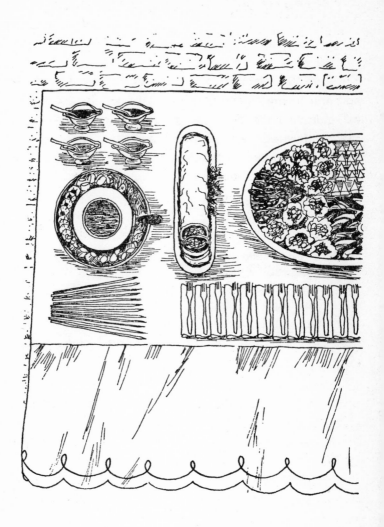

X BUFFET-STYLE FONDUE ENTERTAINING

We seem to have come full circle. Starting in Switzerland and proceeding around the globe to China (which landed us squarely back in Switzerland again), we've sampled practically every variety of fondue cookery. Now I'd like to incorporate our gleanings into several suggestions for fun fondue parties, tossing national barriers aside. I said at the outset that much of the charm of fondue parties lay in their informality, and that the ideal grouping was six or, given two fondue pots and a slightly larger table, twelve.

But we needn't stop there. There comes a time in the life of anyone with a large circle of friends when it behooves him/her to entertain a large group, and this can often cause panic and consternation in the stoutest of entertaining hearts. Let me attempt to dispel both—first with this suggested Fondue Buffet International. One of its special combination charms, heartily vouched for by all who've tried it, is that it combines both the French and Oriental rule of cookery—flavor, texture and color—with the American stipulation: no kitchen cooking on the day of the party.

Is your kitchen small? Take heart. Look at the lot of the airlines stewardess who, working out of the minute galley kitchen of today's jet, dispenses, within a brief time-span, an elegant seven-course meal resplendent with white damask, silver, crystal, china, appropriate wines and a gracious smile. The voyager-recipient tends to believe all this materializes out of thin air. (Understandable at jet altitude!) Not so. It's all a matter of advance planning, and regardless of the restricted dimensions of your home cooking-zone, you can do the same.

Here follow *10 rules for cooking and entertaining buffet-style.*

1. Invite congenial guests. Meaning, people who are likely to get on. Food helps, but inherently, fun is people.

2. Plan the menu (see below), and make out your shopping list, including wines.

3. Check your equipment to see what you haven't got, and make arrangements to rent or borrow it. This may well include a second fondue set, extra china and crystal, and perhaps table linen as well.

4. Before you start to shop, strip the refrigerator of all but the barest essentials. Vital.

5. Shop for, and prepare, one or two dishes at a time so as to avoid confusion in a small kitchen, allowing three or four days before the party for basic food preparation. Salad and antipasto ingredients should be assembled the day before.

6. Keep your shopping list and menu at hand. Cross off each duty as you perform it; each item as you buy it. Make a checklist of *things to be done on the day of the party.* Surely you've not been exempt from the universal experience of finding a special pièce de résistance tucked away in the rear of the refrigerator and forgotten until your party is but a pleasant memory? In addition to your day-of-the-event check list, pencil in a schedule of what you plan to do to put yourself in party shape. Add any and all other last-minute details connected with food-arranging and entertaining.

7. Leave plenty of time to set the table unto the nth detail *before* you get into your party clothes. If space is limited, napkins can be stacked between plates, wrapped around the silver, or folded in the wine glasses. Think through the menu as though you were about to start eating, and place everything in the order of use. As to appearance, remember that with fondue and its accouterments, food is a prominent part of the display and must be considered part of the color scheme.

8. Wine etiquette: Do you enjoy pouring wine? If so, pour it. But if you want to be ultra-Emily Post, prior to the party assign the pleasant and gracious task to a willing male guest or two. Again keeping space shortage in mind, you may decide to arrange the wine bottles and glasses on their own small table. Make certain that you've got extra ice cubes on hand to chill the wine. Have the wine chilled (if it's white or rosé) and waiting when the guests arrive. Be certain that guests have a place to rest their wine goblets while they're eating. (Easier said than done, but it's got to be done.)

9. Put on your most unharassed look, greet your guests, and make them feel welcome. (Have you arranged a place for people to put their coats??)

10. Enjoy your own party!

The menu that follows, I candidly confess, is planned to please men. This is not a dainty tea-party. That's not the kind of cooking I grew up on, and my profession militates against it. Sociologists muse over the fact that the divorce rate among stewardesses is startlingly low. Perhaps part of the explanation lies in the hearty meal philosophy most of us adhere to.

25. FONDUE BUFFET INTERNATIONAL.

MENU

Antipasti: Arrange on one large or two small trays: leaves of 2 large bunches escarole, 60 half-slices hard Italian salami; 15 slices Provolone cheese, quartered; 3 cans (each 4¾ oz.) sardines; 2 cans (each 6½ oz.) drained tuna fish chunks; 3 cans (each 2 oz.) drained anchovy fillets; 1 can (5¾ oz.) drained stuffed green olives; 1 can (5¾ oz.) drained black olives; 1 bunch celery stalks; 24 scallions; 12 hard-cooked eggs, quartered; 12 tomatoes, quartered; 2 thinly-sliced lemons; 1-pint jar pimentos, thinly sliced. Garnish eggs with anchovies; sardines with lemons; tuna with pimentos. Optional: Marinated eggplant, prosciutto, stuffed hot tomatoes, small hot green peppers. Drizzle oil and vinegar dressing over all. Serves 24.

Mexican Chili Dip: (Can be prepared 4 days prior to the party.) In a bowl, mix 12 tablespoons chili powder, 5½ tablespoons paprika, 4 tablespoons cumin powder or seed, 2 tablespoons oregano, 3 cans rinsed sweet peppers, 2 tablespoons salt and 4 tablespoons white pepper. Sauté 1½ pounds ground or finely-diced beef suet in a heavy saucepan about 20 minutes, or until crisp. Remove any pieces not completely fried. Pour suet and fat into 8-quart pan. Cut 8 pounds beef for stew into 1-inch cubes and add to pan with 12 finely-chopped fresh garlic buds. Add spices from the bowl and enough water to almost cover. Cover pan and simmer for about 9 hours, or until the meat is cooked to shreds. After about 5 hours, add 2 cups water and cook for another 4 hours, stirring occasionally. Reheat on the day of the party and serve in a candle-warmed dish with saltines. Serves 24.

Embutido de Pollo (Sausage of Chicken): Grind 1½ pounds boned and skinned chicken breasts and ½ pound boiled ham through the finest blade of a food grinder (not blender). Combine ¼ cup water, ¼ teaspoon salt and ¼ pound chicken livers; boil for 5 minutes. Drain and chop livers. Beat 3 eggs, ¾ teaspoon salt, ¼ teaspoon nutmeg, and ¼ teaspoon black pepper. Add chopped livers, the ground meat mixture and 3 tablespoons cracker crumbs. Mix well and place on a sheet of foil. Shape like a roll about 2½ inches around and 12 inches long. Sprinkle with a few tablespoons cracker crumbs. Using a pastry brush, coat roll completely with 3 lightly-beaten eggs and sprinkle with more cracker crumbs. Again brush with egg mixture. Repeat at least two more times to make a heavy coating. Prepare a white muslin cloth which is wide and long enough to cover the roll. Pour 4 quarts strong chicken broth into large roasting pan and bring to a boil. Sprinkle the muslin with more cracker crumbs. Place the role into the chicken broth and simmer for 30 minutes. Remove roll from the stock, cool *slightly* and remove the cloth (cloth will stick if it becomes cool). Refrigerate for 24 hours; Embutido de Pollo may be frozen up to a month ahead. Cut into thin slices and serve cold. Serves 24.

Sacher Cheese: Combine 1 cup soft butter, 3¾ cups creamed cottage cheese, 9 sieved hard-cooked egg yolks, 12 finely chopped anchovy fillets, 3 teaspoons olive oil, 6 tablespoons grated onion, 1 teaspoon dry mustard, 3 teaspoons paprika, and salt and pepper to taste in large mixing bowl. Beat on the highest speed of electric mixer or divide recipe and whirl in an electric blender. Form into two balls; with a knife score the tops diamond-shape. Sprinkle tops with 9 sieved hard-cooked egg whites and chopped chives. Cover with plastic wrap and refrigerate. Serve surrounded with pumpernickel triangles or tiny bite-size pretzels. Add a side dish of pickled sliced beets. Serves 24.

Seafood Fondue—recipe follows

Assorted Sauces: Tartar Sauce, Lemon-Chili Sauce, Curry Sauce, Garlic Sauce. (See index. Prepare all sauces a day in advance.)

Scandinavian Salad: Combine 8 cups well-drained cooked small green peas, 4 finely-chopped medium-size onions, 4 chopped dill pickles, ¾ cup chopped pimentos and 9 slices diced boiled ham. Salt and pepper to taste. Coat lightly with mayonnaise. Cover with plastic wrap; refrigerate. Serves 24.

Pecan Toasties: Combine 2 sticks butter (½ pound) and two 3-ounce packages cream cheese (both at room temperature) with 3 cups sifted flour and ½ teaspoon salt. Crumble mixture with fingertips until the consistency of molding clay. Pinch off small balls and press into small tart pans evenly across the bottom and up the sides. *Filling:* Beat 4 eggs, add 3 cups firmly-packed brown sugar, 4 tablespoons melted butter, 4 teaspoons vanilla and 2½ cups chopped pecans. Spoon mixture into unbaked tart shells and bake in 350°F. oven about 20-25 minutes, or until delicately brown. Makes 36 small or 24 medium tarts.

French Coffee: See index

SEAFOOD FONDUE

2 pounds fresh lobster tails, cut in bite-size chunks
2 pounds fresh bay scallops, or sea scallops, cut in half
2 pounds medium-size fresh shrimp, peeled and deveined
  Peanut oil, 3 cups per fondue pot

PART I   (IN ADVANCE):

Blot excess moisture from seafood. Arrange on platters, garnish with parsley and lemon slices. Refrigerate until 30 minutes before serving. Pour peanut oil into fondue pots and heat to 375°F. on a deep fat thermometer, or, test heat. To test, brown a 1-inch cube of day-old bread; if it browns in 30-40 seconds, the fat is hot enough.

PART II   (FONDUE POT OVER TABLE BURNER;
USE HIGH SETTING ON ELECTRIC FONDUE):

Adjust heating elements to maintain temperature. Re-check temperature during the party since oil too hot tends to overcook and toughen seafood. Surround each fondue pot with an assortment of sauces. Arrange fondue forks on a small tray within easy reach of each fondue pot.

PART III   (EACH GUEST):

Spears and cooks his own seafood and dips it into the preferred sauce. Serves 24.

26. THE FONDUE COCKTAIL PARTY: HORS D'OEUVRES.

Whatever your private feelings about cocktail parties (and they run the gamut), sooner or later you'll find yourself giving one. They are as inevitable as taxes. So face up, and resolve to give a doozy.

Experience, or at the very least hearsay, has taught us that for total if temporary euphoria, true devotees of the cocktail circuit require nothing more than an unlimited supply of Beefeater's gin, lots of ice, a few twists of lemon peel, and the proverbial medicine-dropper for the ultra-dry vermouth. Thus equipped, they'll carry on indefinitely —until, in fact, somebody has to carry them out.

Notwithstanding, cocktail parties are unpredictable; even the diehards may suddenly discover that they're hungry before total oblivion sets in. And whereas the usual cocktail niblets may lie around untouched, an enticing selection of hot and heady fondue-style hors d'oeuvres could make the day for the less liquor-minded people on your scene—and might even lure those addicted members of the martini cult away from the bar before they *and* your Beefeater's are completely gone.

With these praiseworthy aims in mind, this section will feature some hors d'oeuvre variations on the fondue formula. These innovations don't pretend to be fondues in any classic sense, but they are (a) delicious and (b) novel and (c) a virtual guarantee that your cocktail party will *not* be just another port-of-call on the social itinerary. You may even find yourself stampeded into giving another!

BLENDER CHEESE FONDUE

    1⅓ cups dry white wine, (Neuchâtel, Riesling or Chablis)
    1 pound Gruyère, cut into ¾-inch cubes
    1 thinly sliced fresh garlic clove
    1 tablespoon cornstarch
    ¼ teaspoon freshly-ground black pepper
    ¼ teaspoon nutmeg
    1½ teaspoons lemon juice
    2 tablespoons kirsch

PART I   (IN ADVANCE):

Heat the wine in the fondue pot over medium heat until bubbles rise to the surface. Put all ingredients into blender container, cover and process until smooth. Pour mixture into fondue pot and cook over medium heat until thickened, stirring occasionally.

PART II   (FONDUE POT OVER TABLE BURNER;
USE MEDIUM SETTING ON ELECTRIC FONDUE):

Adjust the burner so that the fondue will simmer slowly throughout the cocktail hour. Heap small trays with an assortment of breads and rolls in various shapes. Small cooked potatoes are also dunkables.

PART III   (EACH GUEST):

Spears bread through soft side of crust, or potato, and dunks it into the pot, giving a good stir each time. Serves 12 as an hors d'oeuvre.

FONDUE STEUBEN

1 pound bratwurst, braunwurst, or weisswurst, skinned and cut
    into ½-inch cubes or use smoked cocktail sausages
1 pound Gruyère, cut into ½-inch cubes
    Peanut oil, approximately 3 cups

PART I   (IN ADVANCE):

Arrange cubed wurst and cheese on platters or in bowls. Pour oil into the fondue pot. Heat to about 375°F. on a deep fat thermometer. If you have no thermometer, test it with a small bread cube. It is hot enough for fonduing when it cooks the bread brown and crisp in 30-40 seconds.

PART II   (FONDUE POT OVER TABLE BURNER;
USE HIGHEST SETTING ON ELECTRIC FONDUE):

To protect the table top, place tray under table burner. Adjust burner so that oil will be heated to the boiling point through the cocktail hour.

PART III   (EACH GUEST):

Spears cube of cheese and cube of wurst with long wooden skewer and dunks it into the hot fat, cooking it until cheese starts to melt. Serves 12 as an hors d'oeuvre.

DEMI-PIGS-IN-THE-BLANKET

1 stick butter (¼ pound)
1 three-ounce package cream cheese
1½ cups sifted flour
¼ teaspoon salt
36 small cocktail wieners
    Peanut oil, approximately 3 cups

PART I   (IN ADVANCE):

Have butter and cream cheese at room temperature. Sift flour with salt and add to the butter and cream cheese. Crumble mixture with fingertips until the consistency of molding clay. Pinch off small balls of dough and flatten with palms of hands to a thickness of ⅛ inch. Mold dough around cocktail wieners, sealing edges well. Arrange on platter and refrigerate until ready to use.

Pour the oil into the fondue pot. Heat to about 375° on a deep fat thermometer. If you have no thermometer, test it with a small bread cube.

PART II (FONDUE POT OVER TABLE BURNER;
USE HIGHEST SETTING ON ELECTRIC FONDUE);

To protect the table top, place tray under table burner. Adjust burner so that oil will be heated to the boiling point throughout the cocktail hour.

PART III (EACH GUEST):

Spears small wiener with disposable skewer and dunks it into the hot fat, cooking it until crust is golden and crispy, approximately 30 seconds, and then dips it in Tomato Sauce (see index), prepared mustard or hot dog relish. Serve 12 as an hors d'oeuvre.

Note: Cooked shrimp can be used in place of cocktail wieners for Demi-Shrimps-In-The-Blanket.

SHISH KEBABS, (Fondue-style)

¾ cup olive oil
¼ cup lemon juice
1 tablespoon red wine vinegar
2 cloves fresh garlic
1 bay leaf
½ teaspoon thyme
½ teaspoon oregano
½ teaspoon pepper
1 teaspoon salt
2 pounds leg of lamb or beef, cut into 1-inch cubes
Cherry tomatoes
1-inch squares of green pepper
Tiny whole onions, parboiled from 5-10 minutes
Peanut oil, approximately 3 cups

PART I (IN ADVANCE):

Combine the olive oil, lemon juice, vinegar, garlic, bay

leaf, thyme, oregano, pepper and salt. Blend in blender and pour over cubed meat. Marinate at least 6 hours or overnight. Drain the meat cubes on paper toweling. String skewers: cherry tomato, green pepper, onion, and meat cube, and set out on large platters. Or bowls holding individual foods can be set on the table so guests can assemble their own skewers.

Pour the oil into the fondue pot. Heat to about 375° on a deep fat thermometer. If you have no thermometer, test a small bread cube; oil is hot enough when it cooks the bread brown and crisp in 30-40 seconds.

PART II (FONDUE POT OVER TABLE BURNER; USE HIGHEST SETTING ON ELECTRIC FONDUE):

Place tray under table burner. Adjust burner so that oil is kept at the proper temperature.

PART III (EACH GUEST):

Dunks a shish kebab into the hot boiling oil, cooking it to his taste—10-20 seconds for rare and 50-60 seconds for well-done. Usually three to four people can cook their meat at the same time. Serves 12 as hors d'oeuvres.

27. OPEN HOUSE WITH DESSERT FONDUES.

You don't want to go full-scale meal, and yet you can't leave it at just a cocktail party—and staring you in the face is the irrefutable fact that you owe invitations to everybody in your precinct. I put it to you that the ideal solution is a Dessert Fondue Open House, because (1) each of the dessert dips and dunkables suggested is delicious beyond description and (2) your hospitality will bear the unmistakable stamp of your own personal touch even if you leave the sandwiches to your local friendly delicatessen and (3) the Dessert Fondue proves to be remarkably flexible: you can fulfill all outstanding obligations to the bridge-and-tea gang in the late afternoon, or to your assorted friends of an evening on a come-to-dessert-after-8-and-stay-indefinitely basis. Nobody is pretending that the Dessert Fondue is an "echt-fondue" classic. Rather, these marvelous bubbling sauces and the accompanying dippables are yet another instance of how the fun, flame and saucery of the fondue scene can be expanded for the benefit of society at large and at small.

(Another possibility is a Chocolate Fun Fondue Party Buffet. See Chap. VI, Sect. 14 for details.)

ORANGE SAUCE

1 cup sugar
2 tablespoons cornstarch
⅛ teaspoon salt
2 cups fresh orange juice
2 egg yolks
⅓ cup Cognac
6 tablespoons butter
1 tablespoon grated orange rind, or 2 1" x 2" strips orange rind

PART I (IN ADVANCE):

Mix the sugar, cornstarch and salt in the fondue pot. Add the orange juice and stir well. Bring to a boil, stirring constantly. Continue to stir. Cook for 15 minutes. Remove from burner and with a wire whisk quickly beat in the eggs, Cognac, butter and orange rind. Blend well.

PART II (FONDUE POT OVER TABLE BURNER;
USE LOW SETTING ON ELECTRIC FONDUE):

Adjust the burner so that the sauce will remain warm without boiling.

PART III   (EACH GUEST):

Spears dunkables and dips them in the sauce, giving a good stir each time. Suggested dunkables—mini-crepes, angel food cake, pound cake, lady fingers, fresh fruits or dates. Serves 6.

EGGNOG SAUCE

1 pint light cream
½ cup sugar
3 egg yolks, beaten
½ teaspoon vanilla
3 tablespoons dark rum

PART I   (IN ADVANCE):

Scald the cream in the fondue pot over low heat. Add the sugar. Remove from the heat and beat in with a wire whisk one egg yolk at a time, beating well after each addition. Add the vanilla and rum. Heat again, but do not boil, lest the mixture curdle.

Note: Blender method. Melt butter in fondue pot over medium heat. Put sugar, cornstarch, salt, orange juice and strips of rind into blender container. Cover and process until rind is finely grated. Add egg yolks while processing, blending well. Pour into fondue pot and cook over medium heat, stirring constantly until thickened. Stir in rum.

PART II   (FONDUE POT OVER TABLE BURNER;
USE LOW SETTING ON ELECTRIC FONDUE):

Adjust the burner so that the sauce will remain warm without boiling. Sauce may curdle if heat is too high. If this happens, reprocess in blender a few seconds.

PART III   (EACH GUEST):

Spears dunkables and dips them in the sauce, giving a good stir each time. Suggested dunkables—Fresh fruits, angel food, chiffon or pound cake. Serves 6.

DESSERT CHEESE FONDUE

    1 teaspoon butter
    4 ounces mild Cheddar cheese, minced or grated
    2 ounces processed Swiss cheese, minced or grated
    1 egg, beaten
    1 cup milk
    1 tablespoon sugar
    ⅓ cup coffee liqueur

PART I   (IN ADVANCE):

Melt the butter, Cheddar and Swiss cheese in the fondue pot over low heat. With a wire whisk beat in the egg. Gradually stir in the milk, sugar and liqueur.

PART II   (FONDUE POT OVER TABLE BURNER;
USE LOW SETTING ON ELECTRIC FONDUE):

Adjust the burner so that the fondue will remain warm without boiling.

PART III   (EACH GUEST):

Spears dunkables and dips them in the fondue, giving a good stir each time. Slices of apple and pear, or cubes of pineapple are delectable dunkables. Serves 6.

MOCHA CHOCOLATE FONDUE

    1 tablespoon butter
    2 1-ounce squares unsweetened chocolate
    1 teaspoon instant coffee
    ½ teaspoon cinnamon
    1 7-ounce jar marshmallow creme
    ⅓ cup dark rum

PART I   (IN ADVANCE):

Melt butter and chocolate over medium heat. Add the instant coffee, cinnamon and marshmallow creme. Stir until blended. Add the rum and stir well.

PART II   (FONDUE POT OVER TABLE BURNER;
USE LOW SETTING ON ELECTRIC FONDUE):

Adjust the burner so that the fondue will remain warm without boiling.

PART III   (EACH GUEST):

Spears dunkables and twirls them around in the fondue. Suggested dunkables—angel food cake, pound cake, marshmallows, small cream puffs and dates. Serves 6.

RASPBERRY SAUCE

    1 box (14-ounce) frozen raspberries
    2 tablespoons water
    1 teaspoon lemon juice
    2 tablespoons kirsch
    Fresh peach slices, lightly sweetened, or use canned or frozen

PART I   (IN ADVANCE):

Blend the raspberries and water in blender or force

through a fine sieve into the fondue pot. Heat until bubbly. Add the lemon juice and kirsch. Stir until blended.

PART II   (FONDUE POT OVER TABLE BURNER;
USE LOW SETTING ON ELECTRIC FONDUE):

Adjust the burner so that the sauce will remain warm without boiling.

PART III   (EACH GUEST):

Spears peach slices and dips them into the sauce, giving a good stir each time. Serves 6.

28a. MORNING COFFEE, FONDUE STYLE: CHOCOLATE FONDUE.

Chocolate Fondue, page 96, 97
Sourdough Doughnuts, page 179

For an en-masse morning meeting of the club members (any clubs); for inviting in the entire parish after a mid-morning service; for treating all your kids' friends' friends some gala Saturday—here is the Morning Coffee Fondue. Treat, dunk, and be merry.

28b. SOUL FOOD FONDUE PARTY.

One of the most recent phenomena is the rediscovery of an American school of cookery almost as old as the nation itself. This is "soul food," which like soul music was created in the South by the American Negro and is more basically native to this country than any other cuisine. New York's soul-food restaurants—and they are increasing—are discussed with enthusiasm at au-courant cocktail gatherings, and soul-food cookbooks are starting to appear on local book shelves.

Try the following menu and call it "a soul-food tasting" the next time you entertain.

MENU

Fried Onion Rings

Skillet Corn Bread: Mix 2 cups white cornmeal with 1 cup buttermilk, 1 teaspoon soda, 1 teaspoon salt and 1 beaten egg. Melt 3 tablespoons bacon grease in a 9- or 10-inch iron skillet (or square baking pan). When skillet is hot, pour in cornmeal mixture and bake in 375° oven until golden and crispy, about 35 minutes. Spread with butter. Cut into wedges or squares. Serve warm.

Watermelon and Cantaloupe Balls

Chicken Livers: Wipe 1¼ pound chicken livers clean with moist paper toweling. Cut in quarters. Dry. Dust with seasoned flour. Arrange on platter garnished with clumps of raw spinach.

Green Banana Chips: Peel firm green bananas and cut in slices ½-inch thick (about 36). Soak in ice water for 15 minutes, then dry well with paper toweling and arrange on platter decorated with a cluster of yellow bananas.

Sweet Potato Cubes: Peel 5 sweet potatoes. Cut into ½-inch cubes. Arrange on platter garnished with thin slices of orange.

Green Cherry Tomatoes: Select unripe cherry tomatoes; wash, dry and arrange on platter garnished with green pepper rings.

Fill the fondue pot half full of oil. Heat oil to about 375° on a deep fat thermometer. If you have no thermometer, test a small bread cube; oil is hot enough for fonduing when it cooks the bread brown and crisp in 30-40 seconds. Keep oil at the proper temperature. (Use highest setting on electric fondue.)

Arrange separate heaped platters of livers, banana chips, sweet potato cubes and green cherry tomatoes around the fondue pot, set on a tray. Nearby have goblets holding bamboo skewers (from oriental specialty stores).

Each guest makes his own selection of foods to be skewered and dipped in hot oil.

28c. A FONDUE BRUNCH.

MENU

Bloody Marys: For each drink, fill a mixing glass with 8 ice cubes and add 1½ teaspoons fresh lime juice, 2 ounces Vodka, salt and pepper to taste, 2 drops Tabasco Sauce, 1 teaspoon Worcestershire Sauce, and 3 ounces chilled tomato juice. Blend in blender or shake vigorously. Pour into wine glasses. To serve on the rocks add 2-3 ice cubes to the wine glass.

Fontina or Fonduta. See index for recipe. Prepare the cheese as directed and refrigerate in plastic bags, in recipe portions, so that you have the right amount for each pot.

Toasted Cubes of Quick Batter Bread: (See index.)

Maple Apples: (Can be baked the day before and reheated at serving time.) Wash 6 medium-large apples, core them without cutting through the stem ends and arrange them side by side in a baking dish. In the hollow of each apple put 1 teaspoon butter. Pour over the apples 1 cup maple syrup mixed with 6 tablespoons water. Bake the apples in a hot oven (400°F.) for about 45 minutes, or until they are cooked through, basting them every 5 minutes. Serves 6.

Coffee

Supplement

1. FONDUE DUNKABLES: SOURDOUGH AND OTHER BREADS AND CAKES

I've attempted, via strategic comments stuck here and there, to give you the entirely correct impression that fondue entertaining is quick, simple, and relatively laborless as compared with the tedious preparations entailed in most pezzaz-type food productions.

But at this juncture in our exploration and examination of the lore of fonduerie, I propose to make things not less bother, but rather a little more so. Please consider the possibility of eschewing commercial breads and cakes, of opening your mind and your oven, and of making your own home-baked breads, doughnuts and cakes for fondues. The results will convince you that the game's well worth the candle.

And the name of the game under consideration here is, sourdough. It originated, insofar as reliable records can be traced, with the Roman legions who brought it to Britain; the English colonists in turn introduced it to the American frontier. Early American bread was sourdough bread, and as each pioneer woman had her own orally transmitted way of doing things, it's never really been nailed down to a standard formula.

In essence, sourdough is a bread that uses yeast as its leavener, with the sun as an additive agent, if you've got some handy. The English settlers prepared sourdough hotbreads for every meal, and had no trouble fitting in a few other mammoth activities besides; be assured you can do the same. If you are a gourmet with a little early American ancestry hanging around the family escutcheon, you may even decide to imitate a forefather and bake your bread on the open hearth. (You are more likely, I fear, to have a forefather than you are an open hearth.)

Fondues and sourdough cookery form an ideal team. To compensate for the lack of the brittle crust sported by authentic French and Italian breads, you can slice your sourdough loaf and toast it lightly. Then you'll have a dippable that the Swiss themselves would be hard put to it to surpass.

I've done considerable sourdough recipe-testing in the company of a pair of country-dwelling friends whose impulse purchase of an antique bread-kneader started them on their distinguished amateur careers as topflight sourdough bakers. And in 1967, Hearthside Press Inc. gave the cause a boost with its publication of a fine treatise on sourdough cookery entitled *Breads and Coffee Cakes With Homemade Starters* by Ada Lou Roberts. It is this starter problem that has baffled the sourdough enthusiasts in the past; the old wives' word on the subject—and I don't mean to discredit it—is that, ideally, one should acquire a portion of some aged starter that's been mouldering since time immemorial. My own Hoosier ancestors at the Halfway-House used hops, no less, that grew on our backyard hop vine; the resultant bread must have been very heady stuff indeed. Other pioneer chronicles tell of using boiled peach leaves to kick off the sourdough fermentation.

So much for pioneer lore; I and my sourdough cronies, after diligent and open-minded experimentation, have fixed on potato as the ideal twentieth century sourdough starter, and we have the backing of experts. Why don't you follow suit? Directions follow. And if preparing the starter *and* baking the bread seems too much work, move on to "Quick Batter Bread." But don't quit without a struggle (which these recipes are *not*); sourdough more than repays your time and efforts.

POTATO STARTER

1 medium potato
1 package commercial dry yeast or 1 cake compressed yeast
1 tablespoon sugar

Peel potato and boil it in enough water to cover. Drain off the liquid and reserve. Mash the potato thoroughly. Add enough water to the reserved potato liquid to make 2 cups lukewarm liquid, and in it dissolve yeast. Stir in the mashed potato and sugar and let the mixture stand, at room temperature, in a glass or crockery container, loosely covered, for 2 days or more, stirring occasionally. When fermentation begins, stir at least once a day. After it's sufficiently fermented, cover loosely and store in refrigerator until the evening before using; then remove it. (Always store sourdough starter in glass or crockery jars—never metal or plastic.) Let the mixture stand in a warm place (85°F.) overnight. (I place mine over the pilot light of my gas stove.)

Renewing the starter: Use the amount required for the recipe, and when the starter is reduced to 1½ cups, add to the original batch of starter 1 cup lukewarm water, 1 cup flour and 1 teaspoon sugar.

Care of Sourdough Starter: Sourdough starters require as much time and care as house plants. After two weeks a dark scummy liquid will form on top. At this point, remove starter from the refrigerator. Pour away the dark liquid and stir in flour and water in equal amounts and 1 teaspoon sugar. Activate the sourdough by letting it stand at 85°F. overnight. (*Note:* Never return the starter to the refrigerator at this point without giving the yeast cells a chance to feed overnight at room temperature.) Then it is ready for use, or deactivate it by refrigeration. The longer the sourdough starter stands, the thinner it becomes. If it becomes too thin, more flour than water should be added so it will be the proper consistency. If sourdough starter isn't used every two weeks, it can be frozen.

My country friends and I treasure our original sourdough starter as much as the women did in the early pioneer days. Frozen starters from this original formula have traveled, at 600 miles per hour, the width of the United States and as far south as Puerto Rico.

I highly recommend the following recipe (from Ada Lou Roberts' book but I use my own starter) for a beginner. It combines commercial yeast with sourdough starter:

BASIC STARTER BREAD

2 cups starter
1½ cups cold water
1½ cups white flour
½ cup warm water
1 teaspoon sugar
½ teaspoon ginger
1 package dry yeast
2 cups warm water
1 cup dried skim milk powder
4 tablespoons sugar
3 cups white flour
4 tablespoons soft lard
3 teaspoons salt
4½ cups white flour

Empty starter from glass jar into large mixing bowl (do not use metal or plastic). Add 1½ cups cold water and 1½ cups white flour. Beat thoroughly. Cover tightly (clinging transparent wrap is good) and set in warm place (about 80°F.) overnight.

In the morning stir the starter thoroughly. Pour off 2 cups and set aside. Pour remaining 2 cups into glass jar, cover and return to refrigerator. Mix the ½ cup warm water, 1 teaspoon sugar, ½ teaspoon ginger and 1 package dry yeast. Set in warm place until foaming nicely. Pour the 2 cups reserved starter into mixing bowl. Add 2 cups warm water, 1 cup dry milk, 4 tablespoons sugar and 3 cups white flour. Beat thoroughly. Add the dry yeast mixture as soon as ready and beat again. Add 4 tablespoons soft lard, 3 teaspoons salt and 3½ cups white flour. Stir until the dough clears the bowl. Spread remaining 1 cup white flour on the pastry board. Turn out dough and knead thoroughly, using a little more flour if necessary to make a smooth nonsticky dough. Return to bowl, grease top of dough, cover and set in warm place to rise until about double in bulk or until dent remains when pushed with finger, which should take about 1 hour at 80-85°.

Turn out dough. Knead thoroughly without using any more flour than necessary. Divide and shape as desired. Place in well-greased pans. Brush tops of dough with lard or butter, or if desired, roll top of loaf in thick layer of flour before placing in pan. Cover with light cloth and set in warm place to rise until dent remains in dough when pushed down lightly with finger. Bake in oven preheated to 375° about 45 minutes for medium-size loaves. This recipe makes 3 medium or 4 small loaves which will round up well above the top of the pan if allowed to rise almost to the rim before being placed in the oven.

Quick Batter Bread

Quick Batter Bread is advocated by experts in entertaining fondue-style who lead an accelerated way of life, but who nevertheless like the luxury of homemade bread without the lengthy procedure of sourdough baking. The leavening agent in the case of Quick Batter Bread *is* a commercial yeast. This delicious bread comes cheerfully to the brunch table with a minimum of preparation; it takes less time making than a trip to the local bakery.

Many New Yorkers, weary of public sociabilities, celebrate brunch as a warmly hospitable, relaxed, daytime way of entertaining friends in their own homes. Served from noon on, brunch gives hosts and guests a chance to sleep late, feed, be fed, and socialize with little trouble and at relatively small expense, and still retain a portion of the day for their individual pursuits.

Eggs are usually the basis of a brunch menu, but why not serve a non-alcoholic cheese fondue such as Fontina or Fonduta (see index)? Brillat-Savarin, noted gastronome, was known to have served his scrambled-egg fondue at breakfast. I interpret his "breakfast" as brunch.

If you organize the menu a day in advance, you can still sleep deep into daylight before the guests arrive.

QUICK BATTER BREAD

ONE-BOWL METHOD:

In a medium-large bowl combine the following:

  1¼ cup lukewarm water
  1 package (one tablespoon) dry yeast
  2 tablespoons sugar
  2 teaspoons salt
  1½ cups all-purpose flour

Beat the above mixture until thoroughly mixed—about 4 minutes.

Add another 1½ cups all-purpose flour and beat until "tired" (says the original recipe). This quick batter bread cannot be overbeaten.

Leave dough in the mixing bowl until it comes to the top or doubles in bulk—about 45 minutes.

Stir down and pour into a greased 9″ x 5″ x 3″ loaf pan. Let it rise to the top of the loaf pan—approximately 30 minutes.

Bake at 350° about 45 minutes or until it is well-browned and sounds hollow when thumped with the knuckle. Remove bread from oven and cool.

Bake Quick Batter Bread the day before, cool, and cut into cubes. Store in plastic wrap. Toast just before serving and place in napkin-lined bowl or basket.

Many sourdough enthusiasts, particularly those interested in organic foods, like to make their bread without the addition of commercial yeast.

The following recipe, *au naturel*, came to me from my grandmother Prichard, renowned for her cooking. Her recipe for sourdough French bread has no relation to the more familiar long narrow loaf from France. This recipe is for a very refined white loaf, a status symbol of the day, which Hoosier farm ladies called "French bread" because they considered anything French to be very "toney."

SOURDOUGH FRENCH BREAD

1 cup potato starter
½ cup milk
2 tablespoons sugar
1 tablespoon soft lard
3¼ cups all-purpose flour

Activate the starter the night before (see directions above). Measure into a bowl the 1 cup of potato starter. Scald milk and stir into it the sugar and lard. Then stir into the starter mixture the sifted all-purpose flour and turn the dough out onto a lightly floured board. Knead it well for a few minutes.

Place the dough in a buttered bowl and brush it lightly with melted shortening. Cover the bowl with a towel and let the dough rise in a warm place, free from draft, until double in bulk, or for about 1 hour and 20 minutes. Punch the dough down and let it rise again to double in bulk, or for about 30 minutes. Punch it down once more and shape it into a round ball. Let the dough rest for 10 minutes.

Shape the dough into a loaf and put it in a buttered bread pan about 9″ x 5″ x 3″. Cover it with a towel and again let it rise in a warm place, free from draft, until it doubles in bulk, or for about 55 minutes. Bake in a hot oven (440°) for about 50 minutes, or until the crust is crisp and well-browned. Makes 1 large loaf.

Note: 440°F. may seem like an extremely hot oven for bread making. However, bread is sometimes baked at high temperatures if a pie tin with the bottom just covered with boiling water is set on the lower oven shelf while the bread is baking. This creates enough steam to build up a crisp crust.

Stone ground whole-wheat sourdough bread is my adaptation of a recipe for buckwheat bread from *Breads and Coffee Cakes*. Cubes of the whole-wheat bread can be lightly toasted and are especially tasty when eaten with fondues made with Cheddar cheese.

STONE GROUND WHOLE-WHEAT SOURDOUGH BREAD

    2 cups starter
    1½ cups cold water
    1½ cups white flour
    ½ cup warm water
    1 teaspoon sugar
    ½ teaspoon ginger
    1 package dry yeast
    1 cup scalded and cooled milk
    4 tablespoons brown sugar or sorghum
    2 cups stone ground whole-wheat flour
    4 tablespoons soft butter
    1½ teaspoons salt
    4 cups white flour

Empty starter from glass jar into large mixing bowl (do not use metal or plastic). Add 1½ cups cold water and 1½ cups white flour. Beat thoroughly. Cover tightly (clinging transparent wrap is good) and set in warm place (about 80°F.) overnight. Wash and scald starter jar and lid. Allow to air out overnight.

In the morning stir the starter thoroughly. Pour off 2 cups and set aside. Pour remaining 2 cups into glass jar, cover and return to refrigerator. Mix the warm water, 1 teaspoon sugar, ½ teaspoon ginger and 1 package dry yeast. Set in warm place until foaming nicely. Pour the 2 cups reserved starter into mixing bowl. Add 1 cup milk scalded and cooled to just warm, 4 tablespoons brown sugar or sorghum and 2 cups stone ground whole-wheat flour. Beat thoroughly. Add the dry yeast mixture and beat again. Add 4 tablespoons soft butter, 1½ teaspoons salt and 3 cups white flour. Stir until the dough clears the bowl.

Spread remaining 1 cup white flour on pastry board. Turn out dough and knead well using only enough flour to make a smooth, nonsticky dough. Return to bowl, brush top of dough with butter, cover and set in warm place to rise. Turn out, knead lightly, divide and shape as desired. Place in generously buttered pans, brush tops with butter, cover and let stand in warm place until light. Bake in oven preheated to 375 degrees for about 45 minutes. Five minutes before the end of the baking period brush tops of loaves with cream or canned milk which will make the crust a rich, russet color. This recipe will make 3 medium-sized loaves.

MINI-CRÊPES

1 egg
1 egg yolk
½ cup flour
Pinch salt
10 tablespoons milk
¼ teaspoon grated orange rind
1½ teaspoons Cognac
1 tablespoon melted butter

Beat egg light; add dry ingredients alternately with milk. Add orange rind, Cognac and butter last.

Use blender if available or strain to remove any lumps.

Allow batter to rest for 1 to 2 hours before using. This batter also tenderizes with age and may be kept up to 4 days in the refrigerator. Makes 20-22 mini-crêpes.

To Make Crepes:

Have batter ready. Line the top of your counter with paper toweling.

Heat skillet slowly over medium heat. Skillet is ready when a bit of butter sizzles immediately upon touching pan. Use approximately ½ teaspoon butter for each mini-crêpe.

Melt butter on skillet. Pour in 1 tablespoon of batter. Holding the handle of pan, roll batter around the pan until it spreads very thin and dries almost immediately.

When crêpe is delicately browned on the underside, turn it over and brown on the other side. Holding the handle of the skillet, quickly turn it over on to absorbent paper. Crêpe should fall out. Use as dunkables for Orange Sauce (see Index for recipe).

Leftover batter may be stored in refrigerator and used another time.

BREAD CUBES FOR DUNKING

The traditional commercial loaf used in the fondue is the crusty Italian or French type. Cut it into slices about 1″ thick, then into cubes about 1″ thick, each with a crusty side. This can be done a couple of hours before the party, so the cubes dry slightly.

TOASTING THE HOMEMADE LOAF:

Cut cooled bread into slices 1″ thick. Put the slices back into the shape of a loaf, then set in a loaf pan, and spread tops with soft butter. Toast in a 400° oven. The outside will be crunchy, the inside soft. Cool slightly, then cut slices into 1″ chunks, each having some crust.

GARLIC CUBES:

Melt ½ cup butter in skillet; stir in ½ teaspoon garlic

powder, or to taste. Cube 8 slices of bread or leftover toast. Sauté slowly, stirring often, in melted butter mixture until cubes are well toasted on all sides. Serve.

The secret of making doughnuts was brought to the colonies from England, and the first ones made by the pioneers were round, a little larger than walnuts. They were raised with sourdough starter, and referred to as "Yankee cakes." (When I first started traveling in England, I was confused by the distinction between "doughnuts" and "crullers." In England today "crullers" are our American doughnuts with holes in the center, and "doughnuts" are round and solid, usually with a bit of jam concealed in the center.)

Old-fashioned doughnuts made with sourdough starter are tender, crisp, and fine-textured. One word of warning, however. They must be eaten shortly after being fried because they are highly perishable.

SOURDOUGH DOUGHNUTS

2 eggs
1 cup sugar
1 cup sourdough starter
½ cup buttermilk
1 tablespoon melted lard
4½ cups sifted all-purpose flour
1 teaspoon baking powder
½ teaspoon baking soda
½ teaspoon salt
½ teaspoon ground nutmeg
   Vegetable fat for frying

Activate starter the night before, using the method

given in the recipe for Basic Starter Bread (see index).

Beat eggs and sugar together. Add starter, buttermilk, lard, and sifted dry ingredients. Mix well. Turn out dough and knead on a lightly-floured board until smooth. Roll to ½-inch thickness and cut with 2 ¾-inch doughnut cutter. Put on greased cookie sheet and let rise for 30 minutes. Fry in hot deep fat (370° on a frying thermometer) until golden brown and done. Serve on a platter and let guests dunk them in the chocolate fondue. Makes about 3 dozen.

CAKES FOR CHOCOLATE FONDUE DUNKING.

European cooks of my acquaintance absolutely refuse even to attempt an angel food cake from scratch. I have been baking cakes, including angel food, since I was twelve, and have never used a ready-mix. It takes just under 15 minutes to separate the eggs and measure and sift the dry ingredients, and then you're ready for all the steps you'd have to go through, even if you *did* use a ready-mix.

When I was growing up in rural Indiana, a cook was judged by the quality of her angel food cake. I suppose a successful one was considered a miraculous accomplishment in those days of uneven oven temperatures since it was generally believed that a sponge cake should be baked for a long time in a *very* slow oven.

Farm ladies used the leftover egg yolks to make a special "8 Yolk Fudge Cake." The remaining egg yolks were used for boiled dressing, which was really Hollandaise sauce. I never heard of confectioners' sugar being used, but it does make a much finer-textured cake.

ANGEL FOOD CAKE SUPREME

  1 cup cake flour, sifted
  1½ cups confectioners' sugar, sifted
  1½ cups (12) egg whites
  1½ teaspoons cream of tartar
  ⅛ teaspoon salt
  1½ teaspoons vanilla
  ¼ teaspoon almond extract
  1 cup granulated sugar

Sift flour with confectioners' sugar 3 times. Beat egg whites with cream of tartar, salt, vanilla, and almond extract till they hold up in soft peaks, but are still moist and glossy. Beat in the granulated sugar, 2 tablespoons at a time, continuing to beat until meringue holds stiff peaks. Sift about ¼ of flour mixture over whites; fold in. Fold in remaining flour by fourths.

Pour cake batter into *ungreased* 10-inch tube pan. After batter is in the pan, use a narrow metal spatula and gently cut through the batter from top to bottom to release any air pockets.

Place cake in preheated (375°) oven. Bake 30 minutes or till done. To test the cake: Cake will be nicely browned and will spring back when lightly touched with the finger.

Invert cake and pan on funnel or soda bottle. Keep the cake in this position until thoroughly cool. It will stay high and handsome that way.

Use the narrow metal spatula to loosen cake around sides and tube. Turn upside down and ease out of pan. Most tube pans have a removable bottom. This way the cake comes out unmarred. Cut into 1-inch cubes for a chocolate fondue dunkable.

No one will ever guess what gives this cake the unusual flavor and moistness—it's creamy raspberry yogurt! For easier slicing, wrap and store overnight.

RASPBERRY TEA CAKE RING

2 cups all-purpose flour, sifted
1 teaspoon baking soda
½ teaspoon baking powder
¼ teaspoon salt
½ cup butter
1 cup light brown sugar, firmly packed
1 egg
1 teaspoon vanilla
1 cup (8-ounce carton) red-raspberry yogurt

Grease an 8-cup tube mold or a 9-inch angel food cake pan. Sift flour, soda, baking powder, and salt onto wax paper. Cream the butter with the brown sugar until fluffy; beat in egg and vanilla. Stir in the flour mixture, adding alternately with yogurt, just until blended. Spoon into prepared pan. Bake in preheated oven (350°) 50 minutes, or until cake tester or wooden pick come out clean.

Cool in pan on a wire rack 10 minutes; loosen around edge and center with narrow metal spatula; turn out onto rack; cool completely. Store overnight, and then cut into 1-inch cubes for a chocolate fondue dunkable.

2. SAUCES.

GARLIC SAUCE

> 2 cups mayonnaise
> 1 tablespoon seasoning salt or salt and pepper to taste
> 2 tablespoons finely chopped chives
> 12 large cloves garlic

Combine mayonnaise, salt, and chives in a bowl. Press out garlic buds using a garlic press or fork. Mix into mayonnaise, discarding large pieces of garlic. Cover with plastic wrap before refrigerating, since the odor is pungent and might permeate the other party foods. Use as a sauce for sea food.

HOT CLAM CURRY DIPPING SAUCE

> 2 scallions, finely minced
> 1 clove fresh garlic, finely minced
> ¼ teaspoon salt
> 2 tablespoons butter
> 1 teaspoon curry powder, or to taste
> 3 tablespoons dry white wine
> 24 clams
> ¼ cup clam juice
> 1 cup heavy cream
> 1 tablespoon lemon juice
>   Salt, to taste
>   Pinch of cayenne

PART I   (IN ADVANCE):

Sauté the scallions, garlic and salt in the butter in the fondue pot over low heat until they are soft. Stir in the curry powder and wine and simmer the sauce slowly until it is reduced by one third. Purée the clams and juice in the blender. Add them to the sauce and cook over very low heat for 1 minute. Stir in the heavy cream and blend. Add the lemon juice, salt and cayenne. Reheat the sauce but do not boil. Boiling will cause the sauce to separate.

PART II (FONDUE POT OVER TABLE BURNER;
USE LOW SETTING ON ELECTRIC FONDUE):

Adjust the burner so that the hot dip sauce will remain warm throughout the meal without boiling.

PART III (EACH GUEST):

Picks up a vegetable, bread stick or chunk of seafood with his fingers and dips it into the warm sauce. Serves 6.

MEXICAN HOT DIP SAUCE

1 medium-size onion, finely chopped
3 tablespoons butter
2 cups stewed tomatoes
¼ cup canned green chili peppers, finely minced
  Salt, to taste
  Tabasco sauce, to taste
1 tablespoon soft butter
1 tablespoon flour
½ cup heavy cream
¾ cup Cheddar cheese, coarsely ground

PART I (IN ADVANCE):

Sauté the onion in the 3 tablespoons of butter in the fondue pot over medium heat until golden. Add the tomatoes and reduce to simmer over low heat until their liquid evaporates. Add the chili peppers, salt and Tabasco sauce. Mix together the 1 tablespoon of soft butter and flour to form a round ball and drop into the simmering tomato mixture. Stir in the cream and blend well. Add the cheese and stir until melted.

Note: Blender method. Blender-grate cheese and set aside. Blender-chop onion, sauté in butter in fondue pot over medium heat until golden. Add 1¾ cups stewed tomatoes and simmer until liquid evaporates. Put remaining ¼ cup tomatoes, 4 medium chili peppers, salt and Tabasco sauce into blender container, cover and process until peppers are finely minced. Add to tomato mixture. Complete as directed above.

PART II (FONDUE POT OVER TABLE BURNER;
USE MEDIUM SETTING ON ELECTRIC FONDUE):

Adjust the burner so that the hot dip sauce will remain warm throughout the meal without boiling. Boiling will cause the sauce to separate.

PART III (EACH GUEST):

Picks up a vegetable or bread stick with his fingers and dips it into the warm sauce. Provide fondue forks or skewers. Serves 6. Note: Both this sauce and the one following, among their several versatilities, can be used to give a cheesy twist to *Bagna Cauda* (Ch. 3).

CHEESE FONDUE HOT DIP SAUCE

¼ pound Italian Fontina cheese, or Emmentaler, grated or minced
1 tablespoon potato starch
¾ cup milk
1 egg yolk
2 tablespoons kirsch

PART I (IN ADVANCE):

Heat the cheese until melted in the fondue pot over low heat. Blend the potato starch with the milk. Stir into the melted cheese until blended and smoothly melted. With a wire whisk quickly beat in the egg yolk and kirsch.

Note: Blender method. Heat milk in fondue pot over low heat. Put cheese and starch in blender container, add milk, cover and process until smooth. Pour into the fondue pot and cook over medium heat, stirring constantly until thickened. Stir in kirsch.

PART II   (FONDUE POT OVER TABLE BURNER; USE MEDIUM SETTING ON ELECTRIC FONDUE):

Adjust the burner so that the hot dip sauce will remain warm throughout the meal.

PART III   (EACH GUEST):

Picks up a vegetable or bread stick with his fingers and dips it into the warm sauce. Provide fondue forks or skewers to dip beef cubes, bread and vegetables. Serves 6.

3. A GLOSSARY OF CHEESES FOR FONDUE

APPENZELLER (Switzerland), pronounced Opp'n-zeller, is made of whole milk and has a deliciously subtle flavor and aroma. It acquires its unique characteristics in a bath of white wine and spices, and is then aged under strictly controlled temperatures for a minimum of three months. Firm-textured, golden yellow, with pea-size holes sparsely distributed.

CHEDDAR (Great Britain, Canada, United States), is made from whole milk and has a yellow-brown surface, cream to deep-orange in color. A firm cheese, it has a mild flavor when fresh; the more cured and aged the cheese, the sharper the flavor.

EMMENTALER (Switzerland) is named after the Emme valley where it originated in the 15th century. In the United States it is known as Swiss cheese, but in Switzerland it's known only as Emmentaler since the Swiss, in literally thousands of years of cheesemaking, have invented countless varieties of "Swiss" cheeses. It is made from whole milk. It was a light-yellow interior with holes that develop in the curd as the cheese ripens; an elastic body, and a mild, nutty flavor.

FONTINA (Italy) is one of the fullest of Italian cheeses, made in the Val d'Aosta, Piedmont. Yellowish, between semi-soft and hard, it is made from ewe's milk, in the same way as Gruyère, and often has a few small eyes. Italian Fontina is considered the proper basis for Fonduta, the famous Turin dish, because it melts easily. (Fontina is also made in nearby Switzerland, but the Swiss variety is preferred as a table cheese.) Summer Fontina, best of its kind, has a slightly smoky flavor, the result of being made in the huts of mountain herdsmen.

GRUYERE (Switzerland), prounced "Grew-yeah," is a firm, naturally ripened and aged cheese with the same chewy texture as its famous first-cousin, Emmentaler. Natural Gruyère is sometimes confused with processed Gruyère, the soft blend of Gruyère and Emmentaler shaped into triangular, foil-wrapped portions, which is a processed cheese and not recommended for fondues.

JACK (United States) is also known as Monterey. Made from whole or partly skimmed milk, it is a mild Cheddar-type cheese.

PARMESAN (Italy) is made from partly skimmed milk. It has a dark green or black surface and a whitish inside whose texture is hard and granular. The flavor gets stronger with age, and very old Parmesan is considered a delicacy.

RACLETTE (Switzerland) is also known in Switzerland as Bagne, Gomser, Valais Raclette or Raclette du Valais, depending upon the district in which it is made. It is used mainly for the special dish called Raclette (see Chapter II, No. 5).

SWITZERLAND SWISS (Switzerland) is also known as Emmentaler. After natural aging for at least four months, the very best is earmarked for export. SWITZERLAND, in bold red letters, is stamped on the rind. SWITZERLAND and the "Crossbow" trademark are printed on the protective over-wraps of delicatessen cuts and slices. (Domestic variety not recommended.)

4. SOURCES OF SUPPLY

Your local gourmet shops and department stores are your best bet, but if you're far out on the rural route or if the nearby emporiums fail you, the following companies will supply information and/or the actual merchandise.

Cheese of All Nations, Inc., 153 Chambers St., New York 10007. *Empire Coffee*, 486 Ninth Ave., New York 10018: Kona coffee. *Iron Gate Products*, 424 East 54th St., New York 10022: "21" Club Sauce Maison. *Katagiri & Company*, 224 East 59th St., New York 10022: bamboo skewers; dashi; egg-roll wrappers. *Switzerland Cheese Assn.*, 444 Madison Ave., New York 10022: all Swiss cheeses. *Trinacria Importing Co.*, 415 Third Ave., New York 10016: coconut cream; grenadine syrup; Indonesian sambals; ginger; kumquats; lichees; sembei crackers; Wessa rice; Kikkoman sauces.

Index